OGC Portfolio Product

C000225295

Release, Control and Validation
ITIL® V3 Intermediate Capability Handbook

*it*SMF International
The IT Service Management Forum

London: TSO

information & publishing solutions

Published by TSO (The Stationery Office)
and available from:

Online
www.tsoshop.co.uk

Mail, Telephone, Fax & E-mail
TSO
PO Box 29, Norwich, NR3 1GN
Telephone orders/General enquiries:
0870 600 5522
Fax orders: 0870 600 5533
E-mail: customer.services@tso.co.uk
Textphone 0870 240 3701

TSO@Blackwell and other Accredited Agents

Customers can also order publications from:
TSO Ireland
16 Arthur Street, Belfast BT1 4GD
Tel 028 9023 8451 Fax 028 9023 5401

The Swirl logo™ is a Trade Mark of the Office of
Government Commerce

ITIL® is a Registered Trade Mark of the Office of
Government Commerce in the United Kingdom and
other countries

The ITIL endorsement logo ™ is a Trade Mark of the
Office of Government Commerce

A CIP catalogue record for this book is available from
the British Library

A Library of Congress CIP catalogue record has been
applied for

First published 2009
Second impression 2010

ISBN 9780113312108 Single copy ISBN
ISBN 9780113312115 (Sold in a pack of 10 copies)

Printed in the United Kingdom for The Stationery Office
P002350702   c12   03/10

Contents

Acknowledgements

AUTHORS

Stuart Rance, HP

Tricia Lewin, independent consultant, UK

Paul Wigzel, independent consultant, UK

REVIEWERS

John Groom, West Groom Consulting, UK

Ashley Hanna, HP, UK

Dave Jones, Pink Elephant, UK

Aidan Lawes, service management evangelist, UK

Trevor Murray, The Grey Matters, UK

Michael Imhoff Nielsen, IBM, Denmark

Michael Nyhuis, Solisma, Australia

Sue Shaw, Tricentrica, UK

HP Suen, The Hong Kong Jockey Club

EDITORS

Stuart Rance, HP

Mark Lillycrop, itSMF UK

About this guide

This guide provides a quick reference to the processes covered by the ITIL® release, control and validation (RCV) syllabus. It is designed to act as a study aid for students taking the ITIL Capability qualification for RCV, and as a handy portable reference source for practitioners who work with these processes.

This guide is not intended to replace the more detailed ITIL publications, nor to be a substitute for a course provider's training materials. Many parts of the syllabus require candidates to achieve competence at Bloom levels 3 and 4, showing the ability to apply their learning and analyse a situation. This study aid focuses on the core knowledge that candidates need to acquire at Bloom levels 1 and 2, including knowledge and comprehension of the material that supports the syllabus.

For further syllabus details, see the current syllabus published by the APM Group at www.itil-officialsite.com.

Listed below in alphabetical order are the ITIL service management processes with cross-references to the publication in which they are primarily defined, and where significant further expansion is provided. Most processes play a role during each lifecycle stage, but only significant references are included. Those processes and functions specifically relevant to the RCV syllabus and covered in this guide are also listed. Abbreviations are given in full in section 1.2.

ITIL service management processes

Service management process	RCV syllabus	Primary source	Further expansion
Seven-step improvement process		CSI	
Access management		SO	
Availability management		SD	CSI
Capacity management		SD	SO, CSI
Change management	✔	ST	
Demand management		SS	SD
Evaluation	✔	ST	
Event management		SO	
Financial management		SS	
Incident management		SO	CSI
Information security management		SD	SO
IT service continuity management		SD	CSI
Knowledge management	✔	ST	CSI
Problem management		SO	CSI
Release and deployment management	✔	ST	SO
Request fulfilment	✔	SO	

Service management process	RCV syllabus	Primary source	Further expansion
Service asset and configuration management	✔	ST	SO
Service catalogue management		SD	SS
Service level management		SD	CSI
Service measurement		CSI	
Service portfolio management		SS	SD
Service reporting		CSI	
Service validation and test	✔	ST	
Service strategy (strategy generation)		SS	
Supplier management		SD	
Transition planning and support		ST	
Function			
Application management		SO	
IT operations management		SO	
Service desk		SO	
Technical management		SO	

1 Introduction to service management

Note that references in the headings are to section numbers in the ITIL core publications, where more detail can be found.

1.1 GOOD PRACTICE

Organizations operating in dynamic environments need to improve their performance and maintain competitive advantage. Adopting good practices in industry-wide use can help to improve capability.

There are several sources for good practice:

- **Public frameworks and standards** These have been validated across diverse environments; knowledge is widely distributed among professionals; there is publicly available training and certification; acquisition of knowledge through the labour market is easier
- **Proprietary knowledge of organizations and individuals** This is customized for the local context and specific business needs; may only be available under commercial terms; may be tacit knowledge (inextricable and poorly documented).

1.2 THE ITIL FRAMEWORK

The ITIL framework is a source of good practice in service management. The ITIL library has the following components:

- **ITIL core** Best-practice publications applicable to all types of organizations that provide services to a business
- **ITIL complementary guidance** A complementary set of publications with guidance specific to industry sectors, organization types, operating models and technology architectures.

The objective of the ITIL service management framework is to provide services for customers that are fit for purpose, stable and so reliable that the business views the IT service provider as a trusted partner. ITIL offers good-practice guidance applicable to all types of organization that provide IT services to businesses. The framework is neither bureaucratic nor unwieldy if utilized sensibly and in full recognition of the business needs of the organization.

ITIL has been deployed successfully around the world for more than 20 years. Over this time, the framework has evolved from a specialized set of service management topics with a focus on function, to a process-based framework, which now provides a broader holistic service lifecycle.

Definition: service lifecycle

The service lifecycle is an approach to IT service management that emphasizes the importance of coordination and control across the various functions, processes and systems necessary to manage the full lifecycle of IT services. The service management lifecycle approach considers the strategy, design, transition, operation and continual improvement of IT services.

The service lifecycle is described in a set of five publications within the ITIL core set. Each of these publications covers a stage of the service lifecycle (see Figure 1.1), from the initial definition and analysis of business requirements in *Service Strategy* (SS) and *Service Design* (SD), through migration into the live environment within *Service Transition* (ST), to live operation and improvement in *Service Operation* (SO) and *Continual Service Improvement* (CSI).

Figure 1.1 The service lifecycle

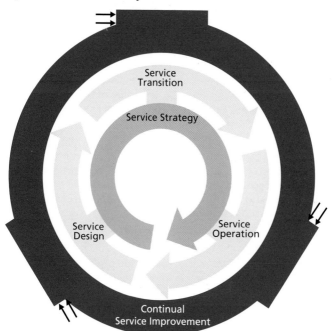

1.3 WHAT IS SERVICE MANAGEMENT? (SS 2.1–2.2, ST 2.1–2.2)

To understand what service management is, we need to understand what services are, and how service management can help service providers to deliver and manage these services.

Definition: service

A service is a means of delivering value to customers by facilitating outcomes that customers want to achieve without the ownership of specific costs and risks.

The outcomes that customers want to achieve are the reason why they purchase or use a service. The value of the service to the customer is directly dependent on how well a service facilitates these outcomes.

Service management is what enables a service provider to understand the services they are providing; to ensure that the services really do facilitate the outcomes their customers want to achieve; to understand the value of the services to their customers; and to understand and manage all of the costs and risks associated with those services.

Definition: service management

Service management is a set of specialized organizational capabilities for providing value to customers in the form of services.

These 'specialized organizational capabilities' are described in this guide, as they relate to RCV. They include the processes, activities, functions and roles that a service provider uses to enable it to deliver services to its customers, as well as the ability to organize, manage knowledge and understand how to facilitate outcomes that create value.

Service management is concerned with more than just
delivering services. Each service, process or infrastructure
component has a lifecycle, and service management
considers the entire lifecycle from strategy through design
and transition to operation and continual improvement.

1.4   SERVICE MANAGEMENT VALUE CREATION

1.4.1   Service value creation (SS 3.1)

An IT service provider has a set of assets in the form of
capabilities and resources that it uses to create IT services
for its customers. Each of its customers also has its own
assets (resources and capabilities) and uses IT services to
enable those customer assets to generate business value.

A customer of the IT service provider only perceives value
from the IT services it receives if a direct connection can be
made between the IT service and the business value it needs
to generate. Therefore, it is essential that IT service providers
focus on understanding, articulating and measuring how
effective their services are in enabling their customers to
achieve their desired outcomes. It is also important that the
IT service provider acknowledges that there is frequently
a difference between what the customer perceives as
valuable and what the IT organization believes it provides.

Understanding the business outcomes and associated business
values that are important to the customer is critical to the
success of the IT service provider and can enable the service
provider to differentiate itself from other providers.

To ensure a common understanding of these values, it is
important that the value of a service is fully described in terms
of utility (increase in performance of customer assets leading

to increased outcomes) and warranty (decrease in potential performance variation). This can change customer perceptions of uncertainty in the promised benefits of a service.

Customers value an IT service when they see a clear relationship between that IT service and the business value they need to generate. The degree of value each customer perceives from an IT service is made up of two components: service utility and service warranty.

Definition: service utility

Service utility is the functionality of an IT service from the customer's perspective. The business value of an IT service is created by the combination of the service utility (what the service does) and service warranty (how well it does it).

Utility can be framed to support the business strategies of customers, in terms of business outcomes supported and associated business constraints removed – e.g. secure operational business processes supported without any constraints relating to business user location.

Definition: service warranty

Service warranty is the assurance that an IT service will meet agreed requirements. This may be a formal agreement such as a service level agreement (SLA) or contract, or a marketing message or brand image. The business value of an IT service is created by the combination of the service utility (what the service does) and service warranty (how well it does it).

Warranty can be communicated in terms of levels of certainty, i.e. the availability, capacity, continuity and security of the utilization of services.

Utility and warranty are not optional components. Both must exist for an IT service to provide value to the customer. Value creation is the combined effect of utility and warranty, where variations in either can be used to differentiate service providers, improving their value propositions and creating competitive advantage.

1.4.2 Service strategy value to the business

Any investment in service strategy must deliver business value in return. These benefits typically encompass:

- Improved use of IT investments
- Tight coupling between the perception of business and IT value
- Performance and measures that are business-value-based
- Service development investment decisions driven by business priorities and clear return on investment (ROI) plans
- Agile adaptation of IT services to pre-empt and meet changing business needs
- Clear visibility of linkages between business services and IT service assets.

1.4.3 Service design value to the business (SD 2.4.3)

The following benefits result from good service design:

- Improved consistency across all services and better integration with infrastructure components, leading to faster and simpler implementation, and improved quality of service
- Clear alignment with business needs, demonstrated through a focus on IT measurements directly related to key aspects of business performance

■ More effective and relevant processes, with improved measurement methods and metrics, enabling informed decision making.

1.4.4   Service transition value to the business (ST 2.4.3)

Effective service transition provides the following benefits:

■ Enables high volumes of change and release for the business
■ An understanding of the level of risk during and after change, e.g. service outage, disruption
■ Aligns new or changed services with the customer's business requirements
■ Ensures that customers and users can use the new or changed service effectively.

1.4.5   Service operation value to the business (SO 2.4.3)

Service operation is the stage in the lifecycle where the plans, designs and optimizations are executed and measured. Service operation is where actual value is seen by the business. The value provided to the business by service operation includes:

■ Agreed levels of service delivered to the business and customers
■ Optimization of the cost and quality of services.

1.4.6   Continual service improvement value to the business (CSI 3.7.2)

CSI recognizes that the value it provides to the business can be realized and measured in different ways:

■ **Improvements** Outcomes that are favourably improved when compared to a 'before' state

- **Benefits** The gains achieved through realization of improvements
- **ROI** The difference between the benefit and the cost to achieve it
- **Value on investment (VOI)** The extra value created by the establishment of benefits that include non-monetary outcomes.

Service measurement provides value to the business by enabling it to:

- Validate previous decisions
- Set direction in order to hit targets
- Justify that a course of action is required
- Intervene and take corrective action.

1.5   THE ITIL SERVICE MANAGEMENT MODEL

All services should be driven by business needs and requirements. Within this context they must also reflect the strategies and policies of the service provider organization, as indicated in Figure 1.2.

Figure 1.2 illustrates how the service lifecycle is initiated from a change in requirements in the business. These requirements are identified and agreed at the service strategy stage within a service level package (SLP) and a defined set of business outcomes.

This passes to the service design stage where a service solution is produced together with a service design package (SDP) containing everything necessary to take this service through the remaining stages of the lifecycle.

Figure 1.2 Key links, inputs and outputs of the service lifecycle stages

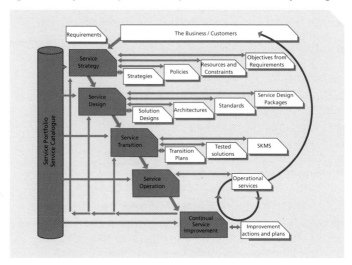

The SDP passes to the service transition stage, where the service is evaluated, tested and validated, and the service is transitioned into the live environment, where it enters the service operation stage.

Service operation focuses on providing effective and efficient operational services to deliver the required business outcomes and value to the customer.

Continual service improvement identifies opportunities for improvement anywhere within any of the lifecycle stages, based on measurement and reporting of the efficiency, effectiveness, cost-effectiveness and compliance of services, service management processes and technology.

The ITIL lifecycle uses models to refine and customize an organization's use of the ITIL practices. These models are intended to be re-usable in a variety of organizational contexts and to help take advantage of economies of scale and efficiencies.

Central to these models are the overarching process elements that interact throughout the lifecycle.

1.6   FUNCTIONS AND PROCESSES ACROSS THE SERVICE LIFECYCLE (SS 2.6, ST 2.3)

> **Definition: function**
>
> A team or group of people and the tools they use to carry out one or more processes or activities – for example, the service desk.

Functions are self-contained with capabilities and resources necessary for their performance and outcomes. They provide structure and stability to organizations. Coordination between functions through shared processes is a common organizational design.

> **Definition: process**
>
> A process is a structured set of activities designed to accomplish a specific objective. It takes one or more defined inputs and turns them into defined outputs. A process may include any of the roles, responsibilities, tools and management controls required to reliably deliver the outputs. A process may define policies, standards, guidelines, activities and work instructions if they are needed.

Process definitions describe actions, dependencies and sequence. Processes have the following characteristics. They:

- Are **measurable**, in management terms such as cost and quality, and in practitioner terms such as duration and productivity
- Exist to deliver **specific results** that are identifiable and countable
- Have **customers** or **stakeholders** with expectations that must be met by the results that the process delivers
- Respond to **specific events** that act as triggers for the process.

Figure 1.3 shows the high-level basic flow of lifecycle process elements in the service management model.

Feedback and control between the functions and processes within and across the lifecycle elements enable the specialization and coordination necessary in the lifecycle approach. Whilst the dominant pattern is the sequential lifecycle, every element provides points for feedback and control.

Figure 1.4 shows the key processes defined by each publication and lifecycle stage.

1.7   RELEASE, CONTROL AND VALIDATION SUPPORTING THE SERVICE LIFECYCLE (SS 2.4)

Release, control and validation forms the core of the service transition stage of the service lifecycle. The following section outlines the key principles of this service transition stage.

Figure 1.3 A high-level view of the ITIL dervice management process model

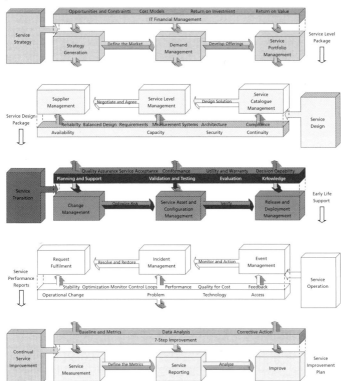

22   Introduction to service management

Figure 1.4 Service management processes across the service lifecycle

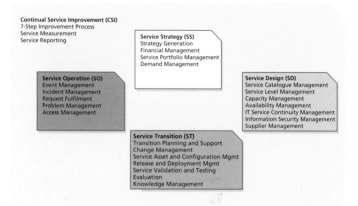

1.7.1   Goals

The goal of service transition is to assist organizations seeking to plan and manage service changes and deploy service releases into the production environment.

1.7.2   Scope

The scope of service transition includes planning, building, testing, evaluation and deployment of all changes to services and service assets. Consideration is given to:

- Managing the complexity associated with changes to services and processes
- Allowing for innovation while minimizing the unintended consequences of change
- Introducing new services

- Changing existing services (expanding, reducing, changing suppliers etc.)
- Retiring services, applications or other configuration items.

The scope of service transition also includes guidance on transferring services:

- Out to a new supplier (outsourcing or off-shoring), in from a supplier (insourcing), or out to a shared service provision
- From one supplier to another
- To multiple suppliers (smart sourcing), partnering or joint ventures
- As part of mergers and acquisitions.

1.7.3 Processes within service transition

Service transition processes are:

- Transition planning and support
- Change management
- Service asset and configuration management
- Release and deployment management
- Service validation and testing
- Evaluation
- Knowledge management.

The rest of this study aid provides more information about the processes that are included in the release, control and validation curriculum. It is important to remember that these are only a small part of the entire service lifecycle described in this chapter, and they should be studied in the context of that lifecycle.

2   Change management

2.1   PURPOSE/GOALS/OBJECTIVES (ST 4.2.1)

Changes arise for a variety of reasons:

- **Proactively** Seeking business benefits such as growth, reduced costs, improved services, or increased effectiveness of support
- **Reactively** As a means of resolving errors and adapting to changing circumstances.

The purpose of the change management process is to ensure that:

- Standardized methods and procedures are used for efficient and prompt handling of all changes
- All changes to service assets and configuration items are recorded in the configuration management system (CMS)
- Overall business risk is optimized (supporting the risk profile required by the business).

The goals of change management are to:

- Respond to changing business requirements, while maximizing value and reducing incidents, disruption and rework
- Respond to business and IT requests for change that will align the services with the business needs.

2.2   SCOPE (ST 4.2.2)

> **Definition: service change**
> The addition, modification or removal of an authorized, planned or supported service or service component and its associated documentation.

The scope of change management includes changes to baselined service assets and configuration items across the whole service lifecycle.

Each organization should define which changes are outside the scope of its service change process. Typically these include:

- Changes with significantly wider impact than service changes, such as changes to business operations
- Changes at an operational level, such as repair to a printer.

Figure 2.1 shows a typical scope for service change management for an IT department and how it interfaces with the business and suppliers at strategic, tactical and operational levels.

2.3   VALUE TO THE BUSINESS (ST 4.2.3)

Change management enables the service provider to add value to the business by:

- Prioritizing and responding to business and customer change proposals
- Implementing changes that meet customers' requirements while optimizing costs
- Contributing to governance, legal, contractual and regulatory requirements

Figure 2.1 Scope of change and release management for services

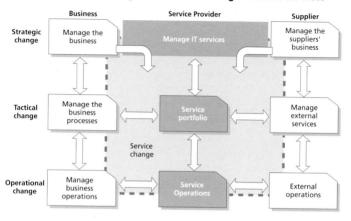

- Minimizing failed changes, service disruptions, defects and rework
- Improving service availability by improving the speed and success of corrective changes
- Reducing the time and effort needed to manage changes.

2.4   POLICIES, PRINCIPLES AND BASIC CONCEPTS (ST 4.2.4)

Change management needs executive support to implement a culture that sets stakeholder expectations about changes and releases. This will help to manage the inevitable pressure to reduce timescales, cut budgets and compromise testing.

Policies that support change management include:

■ Aligning with business, project and stakeholder change management
■ Prioritization of change and management of change windows
■ Establishing accountability, responsibilities and segregation of duties
■ Preventing unauthorized change
■ Performance and risk evaluation of all changes.

Change management should be planned with release management and service asset and configuration management, and the design should include:

■ Requirements (legal, regulatory, standards, organizational practices)
■ Approach to eliminating unauthorized change
■ Techniques for identification and classification of changes
■ Roles and responsibilities (for authorization, testing, Change Advisory Board (CAB) membership, other stakeholders etc.)
■ Communication (changes, schedules, release plans)
■ Procedures for all activities
■ Interfaces to other service management processes (especially configuration, release and deployment, incident and problem management).

2.4.1 Types of change request

A change request is a formal communication seeking an alteration to one or more configuration items. This may be in the form of a request for change (RFC), but it could also be a service desk call, a formal request for change within a project, or some other similar formal communication.

Change management applies across the entire service lifecycle, not just during the operational stage. Table 2.1 provides examples of requests at different stages of the service lifecycle.

Table 2.1 Example of types of request by service lifecycle stage

Type of change	Documented work procedure	Service strategy	Service design	Service transition	Service operation	CSI
Change to service portfolio	Service change management	✔				
Change to service or service definition	Service change management	✔	✔	✔	✔	✔
Project change	Project change management procedure		✔	✔		✔
Operational activity	Local procedure (often pre-authorized)				✔	

Change management needs to support normal, standard and emergency changes:

■ **Normal change** Follows all the steps described in the change management process.
■ **Standard change** Has a documented procedure for meeting a specific change requirement, and is pre-authorized by change management. Examples might include supplying a new employee with standard equipment and service access, or moving a single user's desktop to a new location. Standard changes are often deployed under control of the request fulfilment process.

■ **Emergency change** May be required to repair an error in an
IT service that is having a significant business impact. It
should never be used to introduce new features even if these
are urgently required by the business (these should be
handled by a normal change at the highest priority).
Emergency changes follow the normal change process, with
the following exceptions:

  – An Emergency CAB (ECAB) will review the change, rather
than waiting for a regular CAB meeting
  – Testing may be reduced, or in extreme cases not carried
out, based on a judgement of the risk from delaying
the change.

Documentation updates may be deferred until after the change.
A change process model can help to ensure that a particular type
of change is handled in a consistent way. The model may include:

■ The steps that should be taken to handle the change,
including dependencies
■ Roles and responsibilities
■ Timescales and thresholds for completion of actions
■ Escalation procedures.

2.5   PROCESS ACTIVITIES, METHODS AND
TECHNIQUES (ST 4.2.6)

Figure 2.2 shows the process flow for a normal change.

Figure 2.2 Example process flow for a normal change

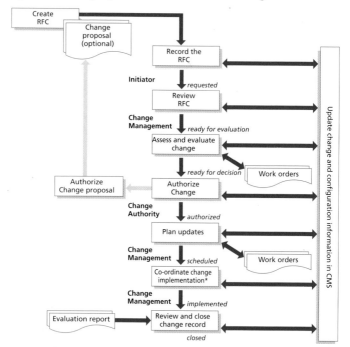

*Includes build and test the change

2.5.1 Record the request for change

The change initiator fills in an RFC, which ensures that all the required information is supplied. The RFC is typically a paper form, an email or a web interface to the change management tool. Information in an RFC usually includes:

- Unique ID
- Description, including configuration items (CIs) and baselines to be changed
- Reason for change, effects of not implementing change, and priority
- Category (minor, significant, major)
- Change authority for this change (usually based on category)
- Date and time, and details of change initiator
- Predicted times and resources
- Implementation and back-out plans
- Impact and risk assessment, including effect on continuity plans.

If this is a major change with significant implications then a change proposal will be required. A change proposal includes similar information to an RFC but in much more detail, with full descriptions and analysis, including business and financial justification.

A change record is created, following a formal process. This record includes the information from the RFC, plus fields used to track the change during its lifecycle. The change record is typically stored on the configuration management system (CMS), and is linked to associated configuration items and to other documents such as work orders.

2.5.2 Review request for change

Change management carries out an initial review and rejects changes that are incomplete, totally impractical, or that duplicate other RFCs (accepted, rejected or still under consideration).

Rejected RFCs are returned to the initiator with an explanation. The initiator has a right of appeal.

2.5.3 Assess and evaluate change

An assessment of the potential impact of the change is carried out. Many organizations have a specific impact assessment form for this. Generic questions such as the 'seven Rs' are a good starting point:

- Who **raised** the change?
- What is the **reason** for the change?
- What is the **return** required from the change?
- What are the **risks** involved in the change?
- What **resources** are required to deliver the change?
- Who is **responsible** for the build, test and implementation of the change?
- What is the **relationship** between this change and other changes?

Responsibility for carrying out the assessment must be defined. Final responsibility is with the service manager and the service owner, who are represented on the CAB.

An impact and resource assessment should consider relevant items, including:

- What impact the change will have on the customer's business operation
- Effect on the IT infrastructure and on non-IT infrastructure, such as security, transport etc.

- Effect on the service and on other services
- Impact of not implementing the change
- IT, business and other resources needed to implement the change, and for ongoing support of the changed service
- The existing change schedule and projected service outage
- Impact on plans for continuity, capacity, security, testing and operation.

Risk assessment should assign a risk category, based on probability and impact of possible outcomes.

The change authority (see section 2.5.4) should evaluate the change based on the impact and risk assessments. They should also prioritize the change based on impact and urgency. A typical change prioritization scheme is shown in Table 2.2. The change will then be scheduled based on its priority, the existing change schedule and release plans.

2.5.4 Authorize change

A change authority is responsible for formal authorization of each change. This change authority may be a role, person or group of people and will vary depending on the specific type of change.

A Change Advisory Board (CAB) should include suitable representation from all stakeholders. The members may meet electronically or face to face and should review RFCs, successful and failed changes, schedules and the change management process itself.

With regard to levels of authority:

- For very significant changes, the CAB may pass the request to a higher-level authority such as a global CAB, or the board of directors
- The change authority for minor changes may be an operations supervisor or the change manager, or other suitably placed person. This authority will be defined as part of the overall change management process
- The change authority for emergency changes may be the Emergency CAB (ECAB), if it is not practical to convene a meeting of the full CAB in the time available.

Table 2.2 Change priority examples

Priority	Corrective change	Enhancement change
Immediate (treat as emergency change)	Risk to life or the ability to continue in business	Not appropriate for enhancement requests
High	Severely affecting key users, or affecting many users	Meets legal requirements
		Response to short-term opportunity
Medium	No severe impact, but cannot be deferred until next release	Maintains business viability
		Supports planned initiative
Low	Can wait until next release	Usability improvement
		Adds new facilities

2.5.5   Coordinate change implementation

Authorized change requests are formally passed to an appropriate technical group to build the change. This activity is carried out as part of the release and deployment management process.

Change management is responsible for coordinating activities to manage the change schedule. This includes ensuring all testing is complete, and implementation and remediation plans are in place.

2.5.6   Review and close change record

The results of every change are reported for evaluation and presented as a completed change for stakeholder agreement. This evaluation is carried out as part of the evaluation process.

A change review or post-implementation review confirms the change has met its objectives. The review includes incidents caused by the change, and achievement of service targets by any third parties involved. Change management (or the CAB) decides what action to take if changes have not met their objectives.

2.6   TRIGGERS, INPUTS, OUTPUTS AND INTERFACES (ST 4.2.7)

Requests for change may be triggered at any point in the service lifecycle, and by many different processes and organizations.

Strategic changes may arise from:

- Legal, regulatory, policy or standards changes
- Organizational changes or changes to patterns of business activity
- Addition of new services or other updates to the service portfolio, customer portfolio or contract portfolio
- Sourcing changes and technology innovations.

Changes to planned services (in the service pipeline) and to existing services (in the service catalogue) may result in updates to:

- The service catalogue, service packages, definitions or characteristics
- Service level requirements, warranties or utilities
- Predicted capacity, quality, value or performance
- Release packages, acceptance criteria or communication plans
- Service assets (including infrastructure such as buildings)
- Processes or plans, such as capacity, ITSCM, test plans etc.
- Procedures, measurement systems and documentation.

Some changes are a result of continual improvement activity; these will also result in an RFC being submitted.

Operational changes, such as server reboots, may be done to correct or prevent incidents. These are often carried out as standard changes. Other operational changes may include requests to reset a password or move a service asset. These activities are often carried out as part of a request fulfilment process.

Inputs to change management include:

- Policies, plans and strategies for change, release, deployment, evaluation etc.
- Change proposals and RFCs
- Change schedule and projected service outage
- Current assets, baselines, service packages, release packages etc.
- Test results, test reports and evaluation report.

Outputs from change management include:

- Rejected and approved RFCs
- Updates to the service portfolio and service catalogue
- Changes to services and other configuration items

■ Revised change schedule and projected service outage
■ Authorized change plans and updated change documentation, records and reports.

2.7   METRICS AND MEASUREMENT (ST 4.2.8, CSI 4.3, 7.1.3)

■ **Output measures**:
   – Number of disruptions, incidents, problems etc. caused by change
   – Number of unauthorized changes (by business, CI type, IT unit etc.)
   – Percentage reduction in time/resources to make changes
   – Percentage improvement in impact analysis, and in predictions for time, effort, cost etc. for changes

■ **Workload measures**:
   – Frequency and volume of change (by service, business area etc.)

■ **Process measures**:
   – Number and percentage of changes that followed correct procedures
   – Ratio of normal to emergency changes
   – Time spent in each activity of the change management process (by lifecycle stage, service and infrastructure platform)
   – Costs against budget
   – Staff utilization.

2.8 TYPICAL ACTIVITIES PERFORMED ON A DAY-TO-DAY BASIS BY SERVICE OPERATION (SO 4.6.1, 8.1)

Change management is described in the ITIL *Service Transition* publication, but many activities related to change management are carried out during the service operation stage of the service lifecycle by people working in service operation functions:

- Raising and submitting RFCs to address service operation issues
- Assessing changes and participating in CAB or ECAB meetings
- Implementing or backing out changes as directed by change management
- Helping to define and maintain change models
- Using the change management process for operational changes.

2.9 ROLES AND RESPONSIBILITIES (ST 6.3.2.3)

The roles of the Change Advisory Board (CAB), Emergency Change Advisory Board (ECAB) and change authority are discussed in section 2.5.4.

2.9.1 Change manager

Depending on the size of the organization, the change manager may be the process owner for the change management process. Some of the following key responsibilities of this role may be delegated:

- Receive, log and assign priority to all RFCs and reject incomplete or totally impractical RFCs
- Decide whom to invite to CAB meetings, issue invitations and agenda, and circulate RFCs in advance for review
- Convene CAB or ECAB meetings, consider advice from CAB or ECAB, and authorize acceptable changes

- Communicate with users and the business, including publishing the change schedule and projected service outage
- Coordinate build, test and implementation of the change, and update the change log with progress
- Review all changes, identify opportunities for improvement and produce management reports.

3 Service asset and configuration management

3.1 PURPOSE/GOAL/OBJECTIVES (ST 4.3.1)

It is incredibly difficult for any IT service provider to be fully effective or efficient if it does not have control, sight and an understanding of the assets that make up the services they deliver to the business.

Service asset and configuration management (SACM) is the process designed to address this need, whilst also supporting and underpinning all of the other service management processes.

The purpose of SACM is to:

- Identify, control and verify service assets
- Identify and record the attributes of configuration items (CIs) and the relationships between CIs
- Establish and maintain an accurate and complete CMS.

The goal of SACM is to support efficient and effective service management processes by providing accurate information to enable effective decision making, at the time required to support the business objectives.

The objective of SACM is to define and control components of services and infrastructure and maintain accurate information on the planned, current and historical state of services and infrastructure.

3.2   SCOPE (ST 4.3.2)

The scope of SACM depends on the size of the implementing organization, but some scoping statements are valid for any implementation scale or objectives:

- Asset management covers the lifecycle of service assets from acquisition to disposal. It provides a complete inventory of assets and who is responsible for their control
- Configuration management ensures that components of a service, system or product are identified, baselined and maintained. It provides a configuration model of services, assets and infrastructure by recording relationships between service assets and CIs
- SACM is accountable for the accuracy of the data within the CMS.

3.3   VALUE TO THE BUSINESS (ST 4.3.3, 4.3.6)

SACM provides visibility of assets and CIs. The configuration model gives clear views of relationships and accurate representations of a service, release or environment. As such it provides business benefit by enabling:

- Changes and releases to be assessed, planned and delivered successfully
- Assistance in speeding up incident resolutions
- Better adherence to standards and regulatory obligations
- The ability to identify the full cost model of delivering a service
- Easy access to information on all assets and CIs held within the CMS.

3.4   POLICIES, PRINCIPLES AND BASIC CONCEPTS (ST 4.3.4)

SACM needs the existence of change management to make it effective. The maintenance of the CMS is the responsibility of SACM, but change management enables the CMS's accuracy to be maintained.

Significant cost and resource commitments are required to implement SACM, so careful thought must be given to the scale and scope of implementation. Many IT service providers focus initially on the basic hardware and software assets, or on service assets that are business-critical or covered by legal and regulatory compliance.

Typical principles include:

- The need to meet corporate governance requirements; for example, Sarbanes-Oxley
- The need to deliver capability, resources and warranties defined by service level agreements
- The requirement for available, reliable and cost-effective services
- The application of whole-life cost appraisal methods
- The requirement to maintain asset and configuration information for stakeholders
- The level of control and requirements for traceability and auditability
- The provision of information for other business and service management processes.

3.4.1   The configuration model

SACM delivers a logical model of the services, assets and infrastructure by recording relationships between CIs. The real power of this model is that it is a single model, used by all parts of IT service management and beyond; it potentially includes human resources, finance, suppliers and customers. This enables other processes to access valuable information so they can:

- Assess the impact and cause of incidents and problems
- Assess the impact of proposed changes
- Plan and design new or changed services, technology refreshes and software upgrades
- Plan release and deployment packages, and migrate service assets to different locations and service centres.

3.4.2 Configuration items

Configuration items vary widely in complexity, size and type. A very complex CI might be an entire service or system, including hardware, software, documentation and support staff. This complex CI could be created from a large number of other, simpler CIs and components.

CIs should be selected using established selection criteria, grouped, classified and identified in such a way that they are manageable and traceable throughout the service lifecycle.

Common categories for CIs include:

- **Service lifecycle CIs** Such as business cases, service management plans, SDPs
- **Service CIs** Including service capability assets (management, organization, processes, knowledge, people) and service resource assets (financial capital, systems, applications, information, data, infrastructure and facilities, people)
- **Organization CIs** Including functional hierarchies, social networks and organizational documentation
- **Internal CIs** Owned within the service provider
- **External CIs** May be owned by customers, suppliers or subcontractors

■ **Interface CIs** Required to deliver the end-to-end service across a service provider interface.

3.4.3 The configuration management system

To manage large and complex IT services and infrastructures, SACM requires the use of a CMS, with a layered architecture. This includes layers for data, information, knowledge processing and presentation.

The CMS holds all information for CIs within scope. It maintains the relationships between CIs and related incidents, problems, known errors, change and release documentation. It may also include data about employees, suppliers, locations, customers and users.

The CMS includes one or more configuration management databases (CMDBs) and definitive media libraries (DMLs) as well as other data. It should provide access to data in other inventories wherever possible, rather than duplicating data.

Automated processes to load CMDBs should be developed where possible to reduce errors, maintain consistency and accuracy, and reduce costs.

The CMS integrates and manages a number of other SACM concepts, including:

■ **Secure libraries** Collections of software, electronic or document CIs of known type and status, used to control and release components throughout the service lifecycle. Access to items in the library is restricted

■ **Definitive media libraries (DMLs)** Secure libraries in which definitive authorized versions of all media CIs are stored and protected. The DML stores master copies of versions that have passed quality assurance checks. Only authorized media should be accepted into a DML, which is strictly controlled by SACM

■ **Secure stores** Locations that warehouse IT assets, such as for desktop deployment. A secure store maintains reliable access to equipment of known quality

■ **Definitive spares** Components or assemblies in a secure store that are maintained at the same level as the comparative systems within the operational or controlled test environments

■ **Baselines** A configuration baseline is the configuration of a service, product or infrastructure that has been formally reviewed and agreed upon. It serves as a basis for further activities and can be changed only through formal procedures. It captures the structure, contents and details of a configuration and represents a set of configuration items that are related to each other

■ **Snapshots** The state, at a particular time, of a configuration item or an environment, for example from a discovery tool. Snapshots are recorded in the CMS and remain as fixed historical records.

3.5   PROCESS ACTIVITIES, METHODS AND TECHNIQUES (ST 4.3.5)

Figure 3.1 shows high-level activities for SACM. This model may be helpful where there are many parties, suppliers, or activities that need to be established.

Figure 3.1 Typical configuration activity model

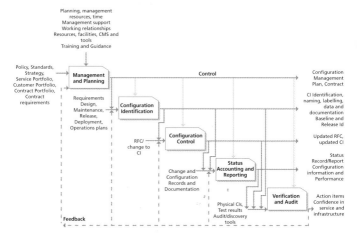

3.5.1   Management and planning

The management team should decide the scope and what level of detail is needed, and document this in a configuration management plan. A typical plan will include:

■ Scope
■ Requirements
■ Applicable policies and standards
■ Organization for SACM
■ System tools
■ Application of processes and procedures
■ Reference implementation plan
■ Relationship management and control of suppliers and subcontractors.

There may also be separate configuration management plans for individual projects, services or groups of services.

3.5.2 Configuration identification

When planning identification it is important to:

- ■ **Define how CIs are to be selected, grouped, classified and defined** The important part of SACM is deciding the level at which control is to be exercised. Choosing the right CI level requires a balance between information availability, the right level of control and the effort needed. CI information is only valuable if it facilitates management of change, control of incidents and problems, or control of assets that can be independently moved, copied or changed. The organization should review the CI level regularly to check that information is still valuable and useful
- ■ **Define the approach to identification, naming and labelling** Naming conventions are established and applied to identify CIs. Each CI is uniquely identifiable by means of the identifier and version. Physical CIs are labelled with the configuration identifier, and procedures are required to maintain the accuracy of labels
- ■ **Define roles and responsibilities of the CI owner** These are defined for each stage of the lifecycle.

The following steps should be carried out during configuration identification:

- ■ **Select the CIs** Make the selection based on documented criteria, and assign a unique name to each
- ■ **Specify the relevant attributes and relationships**
  - – Attributes describe the characteristics of a CI that are valuable to record and that support service management processes

   – Relationships describe how the CIs work together. For
   example, a parent–child relationship; connected to; part
   of; or installed on. Relationships may be one-to-one,
   one-to-many or many-to-one; for example, many
   applications may be installed on one server

- **Specify when each CI is placed under configuration management** For example when it is released, when it is acquired etc.
- **Identify owner** Each CI has an identified owner.

3.5.3   Configuration control

Configuration control ensures that there are control mechanisms over CIs, and maintains a record of changes to CIs, status, versions, location and ownership. Without control of the physical or electronic assets and components, configuration data and information will not match the physical world.

No CI should be added, modified, replaced or removed without an appropriate controlling procedure.

Control should be passed from a project or supplier to the service provider at the scheduled time with accurate configuration information, documentation and records.

3.5.4   Status accounting and reporting

Each asset or CI has one or more discrete states through which it can progress. The list of valid status codes depends on the CI type:

- Valid status for a hardware component might include ordered, installed, in store, working, broken, approved, withdrawn, disposed of

- Valid status for a service might include: requirements, defined, analysed, approved, chartered, designed, developed, built, tested, released, operational, retired.

During configuration identification and control activities, configuration status records are created and modified. Status reporting provides current and historical data about each CI.

3.5.5 Verification and audit

These activities include a series of reviews or audits to:

- Ensure there is conformity between the documented baselines and the actual business environment
- Verify the physical existence of CIs and that the records in the CMS match the physical infrastructure
- Verify that every physical component has a record in the CMS
- Check that required release and configuration documentation is in place before making a release.

Plans are needed to ensure regular configuration audits are carried out, to check that the CMDBs and related configuration information are consistent with the physical state.

3.6 TRIGGERS, INPUTS, OUTPUTS AND INTERFACES (ST 4.3.6)

Updates to SACM information are triggered by changes, purchase orders, acquisitions and service requests.

As the single repository of configuration data, SACM supports and interfaces with every other process, function and activity. There are strong relationships with:

- **Change management** Identifying impact of proposed changes
- **Financial management** Documenting financial information, such as cost and owner

- **IT service continuity management** Awareness of assets that the business service depends on, control of spares and software
- **Incident/problem/error** Maintaining diagnostic information and providing data for the service desk.

3.7   INFORMATION MANAGEMENT (ST 4.3.7)

Backup copies of the CMS are taken regularly and securely stored, preferably off-site to enable access during ITSCM invocation.

The amount of historical information to be retained depends upon the usefulness of the data to the organization. The retention policy for historical records is reviewed regularly and amended if necessary.

3.8   METRICS AND MEASUREMENT (SO 4.3.8)

As with all processes, SACM is subject to regular monitoring and reporting, with action taken when needed to implement continual improvement.

The following measures are necessary to optimize cost and performance of service assets and configurations:

- Improved speed for incident management to identify faulty CIs and restore service
- Impact of incidents and errors affecting particular CI types
- Percentage of under-utilized resources and assets that are re-used or redistributed
- Ratio of used licences to licences paid for (should be close to 100 per cent)
- Accuracy in budgets and charges for assets used by each customer/business unit
- Reduction in business impact of outages and incidents due to poor SACM

■ Improved audit compliance.

Other measures of the SACM process include:

■ Increased quality and accuracy of asset and configuration
information
■ Fewer errors caused by people using out-of-date information
■ Reduced time required to perform audits
■ Reduced use of unauthorized hardware and software, or
non-standard configurations
■ Reduced risks due to early identification of unauthorized
change.

3.9 TYPICAL ACTIVITIES PERFORMED ON A DAY-TO-DAY BASIS BY SERVICE OPERATION (SO 4.6.2)

There are a few activities carried out during the service
operation stage of the lifecycle that directly contribute to the
success of SACM:

■ Informing SACM of any discrepancies found between CIs and
the CMS
■ Making agreed amendments to correct discrepancies.

Responsibility for updating the CMS remains with SACM, but in
some cases staff working within service operation functions may
be asked to update relationships, add new CIs or amend the
status of CIs.

3.10 ROLES AND RESPONSIBILITIES (ST 6.3.2.3)

During the first stages of a project, the programme or project
office may be responsible for configuration management.
At defined release points this responsibility will be passed
to staff working within service transition and SACM will
take over the responsibility for CI documentation.

Roles specific to SACM typically include:

- **Service asset manager** Process owner for service asset management, responsible for planning, implementing, monitoring and improving service asset management as a process
- **Configuration manager** Process owner for configuration management, responsible for planning, implementing, monitoring and improving configuration management as a process
- **Configuration analyst** Works with the configuration manager to plan aspects of configuration management, such as what CIs should be managed and to what level. Trains other configuration management staff and performs configuration audits
- **Configuration administrator/librarian** Custodian and guardian of master copies of software, assets and documentation. Manages one or more CMDBs and/or DMLs
- **CMS/tools administrator** Evaluates and recommends asset and configuration management tools. Monitors tool effectiveness and recommends improvements. Ensures the integrity and effectiveness of the CMS
- **Configuration control board** Defines and controls configuration baselines. Reviews changes to configurations to ensure they comply with standards and other requirements. This role is often combined with the Change Advisory Board.

4 Service validation and testing

4.1 PURPOSE/GOAL/OBJECTIVES (ST 4.5.1)

The purpose of the service validation and testing process is to:

■ Plan and implement a structured validation and test process that provides objective evidence that services match all requirements and can meet agreed service levels
■ Quality-assure service components, the resultant service and service capability delivered by a release
■ Identify, assess and address issues, errors and risks throughout service transition.

The goal of service validation and testing is to ensure that a service will provide value to customers and their business.

The objectives of service validation and testing are to:

■ Provide confidence that new or changed services will provide the expected outcomes and value within the cost, capacity and constraints identified
■ Validate that a service is 'fit for purpose'
■ Assure that a service is 'fit for use'
■ Confirm that requirements for new or changed services are correctly defined
■ Find and remedy errors and variances early in the service lifecycle.

4.2 SCOPE (ST 4.5.2)

Service validation and testing can be applied throughout the service lifecycle to assure the quality of:

■ Any aspect of any new or changed service or service offering, including:

- Services developed in-house or externally
- Hardware, software or knowledge-based services

■ The service provider's capability, resources and capacity to deliver a service or service release.

Validation and testing of an end-to-end service requires:

■ Interfaces with suppliers, customers and partners
■ Defined boundaries of the service to be tested, including process and organizational interfaces.

As well as covering the functionality of the components, testing examines their behaviour in conjunction with their intended use in the target business unit, service unit, deployment group or environment. To accomplish these tests it might be necessary to work with areas external to the service provider, such as public networks.

Testing supports the release and deployment process, ensuring the correct levels of testing have been undertaken, including the validation of the proposed service models as being 'fit for use' and 'fit for purpose' before authorization is given to enter service operation. 'Fit for use' and 'fit for purpose' are defined as:

■ Fit for purpose means being able to deliver the required service utility. A service that is fit for purpose can meet all of its functional requirements
■ Fit for use means being able to deliver the required service warranty. A service that is fit for use is able to meet all of its operational requirements.

Information obtained during service validation and testing can be used to assess the performance of the live system as part of the evaluation process.

4.3   VALUE TO THE BUSINESS (ST 4.5.3)

Service validation and testing provides confidence to the business that new or changed services will deliver the required value and outcomes. It does not guarantee that services will be free from failure.

The absence of sufficient testing can result in:

- Inefficient service management processes
- Increased numbers of incidents and higher requirement for service desk support
- Errors and problems in the live environment that are hard to diagnose, additional costs, and errors that are expensive to fix
- Ineffective use of services, reducing their value.

4.4   POLICIES, PRINCIPLES AND BASIC CONCEPTS (ST 4.5.4)

Service validation and testing is driven by policies for:

- Service quality
- Risk
- Service transition (not covered in this publication)
- Release
- Change management.

4.4.1 Service quality policy

Senior leadership defines quality criteria for an organization, which is formalized in service strategy. The service provider should consider utility, warranty and service level metrics.

The four quality perspectives in service strategy are:
- Level of excellence
- Value for money
- Conformance to specification
- Meeting or exceeding expectations.

4.4.2 Risk policy

The level of validation and testing required will be determined in the risk policy. This can vary considerably depending on factors such as the business's appetite for risk, regulations and safety criticality.

The control required will influence the amount of testing to be carried out regarding service level targets, utility and warranty (which will cover availability, security, IT service continuity and capacity).

4.4.3 Release policy

The level and type of testing is influenced by type and frequency of releases.

4.4.4 Change management policy

The timing of the implementation of changes can affect the approach to testing. The following should be considered:
- Late alterations to release packages
- Automation and re-usability of test-ware (test model cases, scripts and data) and measurement and refinement of test processes
- Integration of testing with the project and service lifecycles and engaging stakeholders in the test process
- Risk-based testing approach.

4.4.5 Test models

Test models help to ensure consistency and repeatability, improving effectiveness and efficiency. Contents of a test model include a test plan ('what is to be tested') and test scripts (including test conditions and expected results). To ensure the test model is repeatable it should be well structured.

Test models use service design and release plans to determine specific requirements. Separate test models can be created for the different types/stages of testing. Some examples of service test models are shown in Table 4.1.

4.4.6 Validation and testing perspectives

The focus of validation and testing is to confirm that the service delivered fulfils all the agreed criteria, including the ability to deliver, deploy, use, manage and operate the service during its lifetime. The service design package (SDP) documents entry and exit criteria for each level and area of testing.

Perspectives to be considered include design of the service, technology, processes and measurements as well as documentation, skills and knowledge.

The service acceptance criteria and associated test plan are typically signed off by the stakeholders that agreed the service requirements.

Table 4.1 Examples of service test models

Test model	Objective/target deliverable	Test conditions based on
Service contract	Validate that customer can use the service to deliver the value	Contract requirements. Fit-for-purpose, fit-for-use criteria
Service requirements	Validate that service provider can deliver the expected service	Service requirements and service acceptance criteria
Service level	Ensure that service level requirements can be met in production environment	Service level requirements, service level agreement, operation level agreement (OLA)
Service	Ensure that service provider is capable of operating and managing the service using the designed service model	Service model
Operations	Ensure that service operation teams can operate and support the service	Service model, service operation standards, processes and plans
Deployment release	Verify that deployment team, tools and procedures can deploy the release correctly	Release and deployment design and plan

Test model	Objective/target deliverable	Test conditions based on
Deployment installation	Test that release package can be correctly installed in target environment in estimated time	Release and deployment design and plan
Deployment verification	Test that deployment is completed and all assets and configurations are correct	Tests and audits of actual service assets and configurations

4.4.7 Business user and customer perspective

The success of a service relies on the involvement of the people who have commissioned and will use the service. Acceptance testing by the business is included in the SDP. The importance of this to the business is that it enables:

■ Measurement of acceptability of the service, including interfaces with the service provider
■ Understanding of the resources needed to undertake the acceptance testing.

The importance of this to the service provider is that it:

■ Maintains business involvement through the lifecycle, avoiding last-minute surprises
■ Manages business perceptions of reliability and usability before the service goes live
■ Provides acceptance test facilities to meet business requirements

■ Improves understanding of the links between acceptance testing and other business activities.

The period of acceptance testing allows the customer and users to become familiar with the new service well before live operation, reducing any initial resistance to change.

4.4.8 User testing – application, system and service

This testing reflects as closely as possible how the service will work in the live operational environment, checking that it provides the correct level of functionality and quality.

The areas that are covered include:

■ Required functionality
■ Changed business processes
■ Service management activities, such as contact with the service desk.

The scope and coverage of the tests are defined in the user test or user acceptance test plan.

4.4.9 Operations and service improvement perspective

Service acceptance checks that the following have been considered before deployment:

■ Technology and facilities
■ Support staff with requisite skills and knowledge
■ Supporting processes correctly resourced and in place (for example, the service desk)
■ Business and IT continuity
■ Access to documentation and the service knowledge management system.

4.4.10 Levels of testing and testing models

Each service asset and component needs to be tested to ensure it meets the business, user and operational requirements before it is used in the live operational environment.

A re-usable test model is developed for each service model and associated deliverables, enabling regression-testing of specific releases for initial and subsequent deployments.

Figure 4.1 shows the V-model, which illustrates how some of the validation and testing activities can be undertaken early in the service lifecycle leading to increases in quality.

Figure 4.1 Example of service V-model

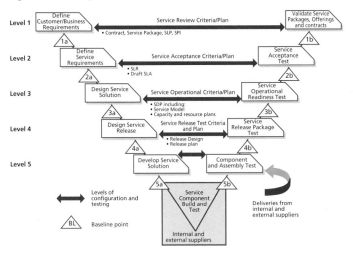

The left side of the V-model shows stages of development; the right side shows related testing activity.

Development of the test model and the test-ware is undertaken at the same time as development of the designs and components to be tested.

The advantages of this approach are:

- Assumptions and omissions are identified early
- Early rectification of errors saves the cost of rework
- Test designs are based on the requirements, not on the solution
- Validation and testing activities are not constrained by tight timescales at the end of development.

The lowest level of component must be built before starting to execute tests. Testing is then conducted in reverse order following the right side of the V-model from bottom to top.

4.5   PROCESS ACTIVITIES, METHODS AND TECHNIQUES (ST 4.5.5)

The key activities undertaken in validation and testing are depicted in Figure 4.2.

Figure 4.2 Example of a validation and testing process

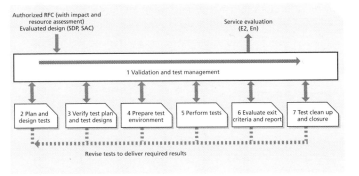

The activities do not have to be undertaken sequentially; several can be done in parallel.

1 Validation and test management

This plans, monitors and controls the complete test lifecycle, including:

- Resource planning, activity prioritization and scheduling
- Management of incidents, problems, errors, non-conformances, risks and issues
- Monitoring and reporting, including collection, analysis and reporting on metrics
- Introduction of changes to reduce potential errors
- Capturing configuration baselines.

Proactive management of activities reduces delays and helps prevent dependencies from being created.

Control is achieved by the use of test metrics which show progress, provide information about earned value and determine the number of tests still required.

Estimation of test completion dates can be derived from good metrics, enabling the best testing to take place in the time available.

2 Plan and design tests

This starts early in the lifecycle and determines what should be considered in testing. It includes:

- Resourcing, including business and customer resources
- Hardware/networks
- Supporting services
- Schedule/milestones, including time allocation for review and acceptance of reports and other interim deliverables, and details for delivery and acceptance of products
- Budgets and financial requirements.

3 Verify test plan and test designs

This is undertaken to ensure that the test model provides:

- Appropriate test coverage for the level of risk
- Coverage of integration and interface aspects
- Examination of the accuracy and completeness of test scripts.

4 Prepare test environment

A test environment is a controlled environment used to test configuration items, builds, IT services, processes etc.

This should be created with the assistance of the release and deployment management process using build and test environment staff. A configuration baseline should be taken once the initial test environment has been created.

5 Perform tests

Tests can be automated or executed manually. Recording should take place to measure tests that have run successfully and to raise incidents for test failures, for creating a resolution or known error.

Any updates will be retested, preferably by the same tester.

The deliverables from the activity are:

- Actual results with reference to the tests undertaken
- Outstanding problems, issues, risks etc. awaiting resolution
- Resolved problems, issues, risks etc. and associated changes
- Testing sign-off.

6 Evaluate exit criteria and report

This activity matches the actual result of the testing phase against the expected result and identifies differences that would:

- Increase the risk to the business or service provider
- Change the projected value.

Examples of exit criteria are:

- The functionality provided matches the business requirements
- Quality requirements are met
- Configuration baselines are captured.

7 Test clean up and closure

Ensure that test environments are cleaned up or initialized. Review the testing approach and identify improvements.

4.6 TRIGGERS, INPUTS, OUTPUTS AND INTERFACES (ST 4.5.6)

4.6.1 Trigger

Testing activities are scheduled in test, release or quality assurance plans.

4.6.2 Inputs

- **Service package** Core service package and re-usable components (could be services)
- **Service level package** Defines the required level of utility and warranty
- **Service provider interface definition** Interfaces that require testing at the boundary of the service
- **Service design package** Including the service model and service operations plans
- **Acceptance criteria** For all levels at which testing is planned.

4.6.3 Outputs

A report is passed to evaluation providing details of:

- The configuration baseline of the test environment
- Testing that was carried out and the results
- Risks identified when comparing expected and actual results.

This information is used to evaluate the progression of the service from before deployment, through early life support to normal operation.

Additional outputs are:

- Data, information and knowledge
- Test incident, problem and error records
- Ideas for improvement of testing process and service design outputs.

4.6.4   Interfaces to other lifecycle stages

Testing supports all release and deployment steps within service transition.

Successful testing also requires interfaces with:

- Service design, to ensure designs are testable and support testing activities
- Continual service improvement, to provide feedback about failures and areas where improvement would be beneficial
- Service operation, for handover of changed maintenance tests.

4.7   INFORMATION MANAGEMENT (ST 4.5.7)

Service validation and testing benefits from the ability to re-use tests. To facilitate re-use, the test management group should be responsible for creating, cataloguing and maintaining test-ware. The use of CAST (computer-aided software testing) tools can also be beneficial.

Information is required on the following, to ensure realistic testing can take place:

- **Test data** Including appropriate test conditions and environmental aspects
- **Test environments** Wider impacts should be considered for significant change. The service knowledge management system and CMS assist the assessment which leads to:
  - Consequential update of the test data

- Requirements for additional test data and environments
- Redundancy of test data or environments
- Testing restrictions due to inability to upgrade test data and environment to reflect the changes

■ **Active maintenance of test data** To ensure clear distinction between test and live data, adherence to Data Protection regulations and use of known baselines.

4.8   METRICS AND MEASUREMENT (ST 4.5.8)

There are two important types of measurement in this area: the measurement of value added to the business, and the internal measurement of the service validation and testing process.

4.8.1   Value to the business

Effectiveness of testing will be judged by:

■ Early validation, correction and confirmation of the predicted value
■ Reduction of incidents in newly transitioned services and of testing delays
■ Involvement of the business and better use and understanding of resources and costs
■ Better mutual understanding of the new or changed services
■ Key stakeholder roles and responsibilities clearly defined.

Economy of the testing process may be measured by:

■ Rates for the key activities (test planning, preparation, execution)
■ Analysis of testing by service lifecycle stage
■ Efficiency of all testing phases
■ Cost related to testing.

4.8.2 Internal measurements

To determine the efficiency and effectiveness of the process, the following need to be considered:

- Test environment set-up costs
- Effort required for defect detection
- Repeat error reductions
- Reduction of new errors found in the latter stages of testing or live operation
- Re-use of test-ware (including test data)
- Reduction in the percentage of:
  - Errors recorded by lifecycle stage
  - Identified errors released into live operation
  - Errors that could have been identified in testing
- Increase in percentage of faults found and known errors documented in early stages of testing.

4.9 ROLES AND RESPONSIBILITIES (ST 6.3.2.6, 6.3.2.11)

There are three roles associated with service validation and testing: service test manager, test support, and build and test environment manager.

4.9.1 Service test manager

Responsible for the test support and test teams, and reports to the service transition manager. This role must be separate from the release and deployment manager to ensure that testing is independent.

Responsibilities include definition of the test strategy, design and planning of test-ware, allocation of resources, adherence to standards, management reporting, test incident and environment management, liaison with the release team, and administration of test assets and components.

4.9.2 Test support

Responsible for independent testing of all components provided via service transition. Some required activities are not carried out directly by the test team. To achieve this, the following are required:

- **Test analysts** Test according to the test plans
- **Developers/suppliers** Responsible for determining root cause of test failures
- **Test design** Undertaken by service design staff as part of the service design lifecycle stage
- **Customers and users** Undertake acceptance testing.

4.9.3 Build and test environment management

Responsible for creation, maintenance and allocation of the test environments, ensuring that resources are being used to the maximum effect.

Key responsibilities are:

- Planning the acquisition, build and maintenance of the infrastructure
- Building the infrastructure to the design specification
- Building and maintenance of test environments
- Ensuring that all build components are from controlled sources
- Integration of application software and infrastructure build
- Documenting build and test environments for handover to service operation staff.

5 Release and deployment management

5.1 PURPOSE/GOAL/OBJECTIVES (ST 4.4.1)

The purpose of release and deployment management is to:

- Agree release and deployment plans with all stakeholders
- Ensure that organization and stakeholder change is managed
- Ensure each release is tested, verified, installed and backed out as required
- Record and manage deviations, risks and issues
- Ensure transfer of knowledge and skills to business and IT as appropriate.

The goal of release and deployment management is to deploy releases and establish effective use of the services to deliver value to customers.

The objectives of release and deployment management include:

- Comprehensive plans that support customer and business change projects
- Releases that can be built, installed, tested and deployed efficiently and on time
- New or changed services that can meet agreed requirements
- Minimal unpredicted impact on services and on the IT organization.

5.2   SCOPE (ST 4.4.2)

The scope of release and deployment management includes the processes, systems and functions needed to package, build, test and deploy releases; in order to establish the service specified in the service design package.

5.3   VALUE TO THE BUSINESS (ST 4.4.3)

Release and deployment management provides value to the business by:

■ Delivering change faster, with optimized cost and risk
■ Assuring that users are able to use new or changed services to support business goals
■ Improving consistency and auditability of service transitions.

5.4   POLICIES, PRINCIPLES AND BASIC CONCEPTS (ST 4.4.4)

5.4.1   Release unit

A release unit is one or more CIs that are normally released together. Examples of release units are a complete application; a single software module; a single web page; or a desktop computer that comes fully configured with hardware, operating system, and standard applications. Each release unit must be uniquely identified using a naming convention that is defined in the release policy.

The decision about what is an appropriate release unit is based on:

■ Time and resources needed to build, test, distribute and implement
■ Complexity of interfaces with other components

■ Availability of resources in the test environment, and frequency and ease of change.

5.4.2   Release design options

The components to be released, and the approach to be taken, are defined in the SDP. Common options include:

■ **'Big bang' vs phased**
  - **Big bang** The release is deployed to all users in one operation. Often used when the same version must be in place in all locations
  - **Phased** The release is deployed to different users/servers/ places using a scheduled roll-out. Introduces the release in stages to reduce risk and make rollback easier. Can also deploy part of the release (such as hardware upgrades) to all users and then deploy other parts

■ **Push vs pull**
  - **Push** Deployment is managed from a central location. This is typically used for a big-bang deployment but can also be used with a phased approach
  - **Pull** Users control the deployment timing. For example, virus signature updates may be pulled by the locally installed application

■ **Automated vs manual**
  - **Automated** Ensures repeatability, but takes time to design and implement. Many activities can be automated, including discovery, build, baselines, comparison of live to expected, updates to CMS
  - **Manual** May not always be possible due to scalability and reliability. Must monitor and measure the impact and error rates.

Each release package can be a single release unit, or a structured set of release units. Release packages should be designed so that release units can be removed if they cause issues in testing.

Release and deployment models help to achieve consistency and repeatability. They should include:

■ How to build the release package and the target environments
■ Exit and entry criteria for each stage, including handover activities
■ Roles and responsibilities, template schedules and supporting systems and tools.

Each release and deployment model should include all activities needed to plan, package, build, test, deploy and implement the release.

5.5   PROCESS ACTIVITIES, METHODS AND TECHNIQUES (ST 4.4.5)

5.5.1   Planning

5.5.1.1   Release and deployment plans

Release and deployment plans should be based on overall service transition plans, use a release model, and be authorized by change management. They should define:

■ Scope and content of the release
■ Risk assessment and risk profile for the release
■ Stakeholders affected by the release, and approvers for the change request(s)
■ Team responsible for release, resources needed, and approach to be taken.

5.5.1.2 Pass/fail criteria

Criteria must be defined for each authorization point, and must be published to stakeholders to set expectations. An example of a pass situation is:

- All tests completed successfully. Evaluation report and RFC signed off.

Examples of fail situations include:

- Insufficient resources to pass to next stage. For example, insufficient money or automated build not possible so risk is too high
- Service operation does not have required capabilities
- Design does not conform to operational standards
- Service acceptance criteria not met or incidents, problems, or risks at higher than expected levels.

5.5.1.3 Build and test

Build and test planning includes:

- Developing build plans from the SDP and design specifications
- Establishing logistics, lead times and build times to create environments
- Scheduling activities and testing the procedures for build and test
- Assigning resources, roles and responsibilities
- Defining and agreeing entry and exit criteria for build and test.

The V-model (shown in Figure 4.1) represents the relationship between building and testing activities. At each build stage on the left, the testing personnel from the right are involved. For example, service acceptance tests are defined when service requirements are defined.

The V-model is associated with the waterfall development lifecycle, but it can be used with other lifecycles such as prototyping and rapid application development. It includes five levels of build configuration, and corresponding tests, as shown in Table 5.1.

Table 5.1 The five levels of build configuration

Level	Deliverable	Testing
Level 1 Customer/business needs	Customer contract, based on service portfolio and service level package	**Service test and evaluation** The service can support business needs (it is fit for purpose and fit for use)
Level 2 Service requirements	Service capability and resources to deliver to SLA	**Service test** Service acceptance criteria can be met. Service can deliver service level requirements
Level 3 Service solution	Solution/system required to deliver the capabilities, including management and operation	**Service operational readiness test** Integration and operation of the capability and resources. Organization and people are prepared

Level	Deliverable	Testing
Level 4 Service release	Release package	**Service release test** Service components can be integrated and release can be installed, built and tested
Level 5 Component and assemblies	Components or assembly of components	**Component and assembly test** Component or assembly matches its specification

5.5.1.4 Planning pilots

Pilots test the service with some users before rolling it out to the whole user base. The scope of the pilot must be planned to provide enough testing with acceptable time and resources, and must include all stakeholders. Multiple pilots may be needed to support diverse organizations, or a range of different trialling options.

A pilot must collect feedback from users, customers, suppliers, and support staff. It should also include analysis of service desk calls, capacity, availability and other data on use and effectiveness.

The pilot should always be rolled back before the full roll-out of the new service, to ensure that a consistent release is deployed.

5.5.1.5   Planning release packaging and build

This should include developing mechanisms, plans and procedures for:

- Verifying entry/exit criteria
- Managing stakeholder change and communication, training people, transferring knowledge, and developing service management capability
- Ensuring that agreements and contracts are in place
- Agreeing schedules and developing procedures to build and deploy the release and manage licences
- Converting users and systems (including any required data migrations).

5.5.1.6   Deployment planning

Planners should be able to answer the following questions:

- What needs to be deployed? (The components and the business drivers for these)
- Who are the users? (Any special language or training needs)
- Where are the users? (Are any users remote or mobile?)
- Who else needs to be prepared in advance? (Service desk, support staff)
- When does deployment need to be completed?
- What is the current service provider capability? (Systems, infrastructure, capacity etc.)

5.5.1.7   Logistics and delivery planning

This stage includes planning for when and how each release unit or service component will be delivered. It requires planning for:

- Lead times and how delays will be managed
- Checking components on delivery and secure storage
- Managing customs or other internationalization issues
- Decommissioning redundant hardware, licences, contracts etc.

■ Resources needed for any parallel running.

5.5.1.8 Financial/commercial planning

Before the deployment starts, it may be necessary to check:

■ Working capital – are sufficient funds available?
■ Contracts, licences and intellectual property, including third-party software and rights to documentation
■ Funding for supporting services.

5.5.2 Preparation for build, test and deployment

Before authorizing the build and test stage:

■ An independent evaluation should be carried out to ensure the service will deliver the required outcomes (see Chapter 7)
■ People and other resources should be assigned
■ Training should be carried out for release, deployment, build and test teams.

5.5.3 Build and test

It is important to manage common services and infrastructure carefully, as they can have a significant impact. This includes build and test environments and management of configurations.

Configuration baselines must be recorded in the CMS before and after build, installation or deployment. Release packages must be placed in the DML and must always be taken from the DML.

Procedures and documents are needed to manage the build and test. These should include:

■ Contracts, agreements, purchase requests, fulfilment, goods in etc.
■ Health and safety guidelines, and security policies and procedures

- Management of licensing and intellectual property rights
- Acceptance and authorization
- Documentation for handover to service operation.

All CIs must be of a known quality. They should come from a catalogue of standard components, or an RFC should be raised to assess the CI and add it to the catalogue or accept it as an exception. CIs are acquired (possibly via procurement), recorded (via SACM) and checked. Verification of components includes:

- Establishing that they are genuine and have been properly acquired
- Checking that standard naming and labelling conventions have been applied
- Checking items against descriptions and documentation
- Checking that appropriate quality reviews have taken place
- Checking software for malicious additions such as viruses
- Ensuring that all changes have been approved by change management
- Ensuring appropriate use of the DML and CMS
- Managing the return of components that are not satisfactory.

The key activities to build a release package are:

- Assemble and integrate components in a controlled, reproducible way
- Create documentation for build and release
- Install and verify the release package and take a baseline
- Inform relevant parties that the release package is available for installation.

Dedicated environments are needed for release, build and test, and they must be controlled and managed using service management best practices. Automating the installation of systems and applications reduces dependency on people and streamlines the process.

5.5.4 Service testing and pilots

Testing will be based on a test strategy and test model.

New business or technical circumstances may need changes to acceptance criteria or service packages. These will need service design input and business agreement, and will include changes to testing to meet the new requirements.

There are many different types of test, including:

- **Service release test** Can the release be installed, built and tested?
- **Service operations readiness test** Can the service be released? Is the business capable of using the service? Are the service teams capable of operating the service?
  - **Deployment readiness test** Can the service be deployed correctly?
  - **Service management test** Measurement, monitoring and reporting
  - **Service operations test** Can the service be operated?
  - **Service level test** Can service level requirements be delivered?
  - **User test** Can users access and use the service correctly?
  - **Service provider interface test** Are interfaces working correctly?
  - **Deployment verification test** Was everything deployed correctly to each target?
- **Service rehearsal** A simulation of as much of the service as possible in a practice session, just before deployment. It can be time-consuming and extensive, but may identify errors or unworkable procedures. Typically uses a full Plan–Do–Check–Act cycle for a one-day rehearsal.

■ **Pilot** Real users and operations, but a limited number of people. Should check enough of the service to verify both utility and warranty. Should include training, documentation, and all stakeholder interaction.

5.5.5 Plan and prepare for deployment, and perform transfer, deployment and retirement

These stages include preparing for organizational change, assigning deployment activities to specific people, and actually carrying out the deployment. Figure 5.1 shows a typical set of deployment activities.

5.5.6 Verify deployment

During this stage, checks are made to verify the deployment:

■ Does the new configuration baseline match the planned configuration?
■ Are documentation updates correct?
■ Are required communication and learning materials ready for distribution?
■ Have roles been assigned? Are people prepared to operate and use the service? Do they have the information they need?
■ Are measurement and reporting in place?

Figure 5.1 Example of a set of deployment activities

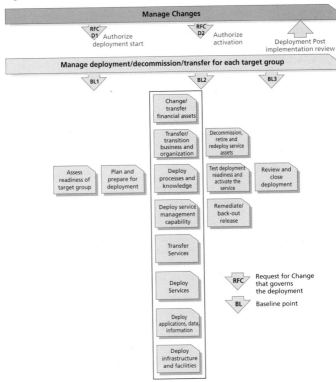

5.5.7   Early life support

During this stage, checks are carried out to ensure that all agreed service levels are being met. Performance data is collected and compared with targets. Service reports are created and issues are addressed. Early life support does not end until the agreed exit criteria have been met. These typically include:

- Users can use the service effectively and efficiently for business activities
- Service and process owners can manage and operate the service as agreed
- Progress is being made towards delivering the expected benefits
- SLAs are signed off and service levels are being consistently achieved
- Training, knowledge transfer, documentation and deliverables are signed off.

NOTE: Early life support is sometimes confused with provision of additional technical support for managing incidents and problems. Although this may be done during early life support, the key aspect is collecting performance data to verify that the service is able to meet all agreed service levels.

5.5.8   Review and close deployment, review and close service transition

The final stages are formal reviews to ensure that:

- All outstanding issues have been documented and addressed
- Opportunities for improvement have been captured.

5.6 TRIGGERS, INPUTS, OUTPUTS AND INTERFACES (ST 4.4.6)

Release and deployment always starts with an approved RFC.

Inputs to the process include:

- One or more authorized RFCs
- Service package, service level package (SLP), service design package and service acceptance criteria
- Service management plans and standards
- Release policy and release design from service design
- Release and deployment models, and template plans
- Entry and exit criteria for each stage of release and deployment.

Outputs include:

- Release and deployment plan
- Updated service catalogue and new or changed documentation
- Updates to SLPs, service models, SLAs, OLAs and contracts
- New, tested service capability, including organizational changes, applications, data, infrastructure, environment etc.
- Updated CMDB with full audit trail of new or changed CIs
- Updated service management plans (for example, capacity plan, continuity plan)
- Service transition report.

5.7 INFORMATION MANAGEMENT (ST 4.4.7)

Release and deployment management makes extensive use of the CMS, including updates for:

- New or changed CIs, including ownership, status, attributes and relationships
- New or changed locations or users

- Plans and records for installation, build, logistics, delivery, validation and testing, deployment, and training
- Known errors.

5.8   ROLES AND RESPONSIBILITIES
(ST 6.3.2.7, 6.3.2.8, 6.3.2.9, 6.3.2.10)

The role of the release and deployment manager is described here. The role of the service test manager is described in section 4.9.1. These roles must be undertaken by different people to ensure that testing is independent. Both roles report to the service transition manager.

5.8.1   Release and deployment manager

The process owner for release and deployment management is responsible for planning, design, build, configuration and testing of all software and hardware to create a release package. This includes:

- Managing all aspects of the release process, including policy and procedures, management reporting etc.
- Managing and coordinating teams for build and test environment and release
- All activities from design of the release to acceptance by the business.

Many of these responsibilities will be delegated to other teams or managers.

5.8.2   Release packaging and build

The release packaging and build manager typically reports to the release and deployment manager and has the following responsibilities:

- To establish the knowledge, information, hardware, software and infrastructure needed for the release
- To build and test the final release (prior to independent testing)
- To report outstanding known errors and provide input to final sign-off.

5.8.3 Deployment

Deployment staff deal with the final physical delivery of the service. They coordinate documentation and communications, and provide technical and application guidance and support.

5.8.4 Early life support

Early life support starts a long time before the service enters operational status. Early life support staff are responsible for:

- Ensuring delivery and quality of user and support documentation
- Embedding all activities required for the service to be operated and maintained
- Providing initial performance reporting and risk assessment of performance
- Providing initial support for incidents and errors.

5.9 CHALLENGES, CRITICAL SUCCESS FACTORS AND RISKS (ST 4.4.9)

Challenges for release and deployment management include:

- Developing standard measures across many projects and suppliers
- Managing schedule delays caused by projects and suppliers
- Understanding diverse stakeholder perspectives

- Understanding risks and building a risk management culture.

Critical success factors for release and deployment management include:

- Building the new or changed service in the target environment
- Testing the service and proving it in pilot deployments
- Creating re-usable test models for regression testing future releases.

Risks to successful release and deployment management include:

- Poorly defined scope and understanding of dependencies
- Staff who are not dedicated and have other responsibilities
- Inadequate management, policies or leadership
- Insufficient finance or delays in provision of money
- Insufficient control of changes, or poor implementation or back-out plans
- Technology limitations or issues.

6 Request fulfilment

6.1 PURPOSE AND SCOPE (SO 4.3.1, 4.3.2)

Request fulfilment is the process for dealing with service requests from users.

> **Definition: service request**
>
> A request from a user for information or advice, or for a standard change, or to provide standard services for a new user. Service requests are usually handled by a service desk and do not require an RFC to be submitted.

Many service requests are actually small changes – for example, a request to change a password, a request to install an application on a PC, or a request for supplies to be added to a printer – but their scale, low cost and risk, and high frequency mean that they are better handled by a separate process, rather than being allowed to congest the normal incident and change management processes.

The purpose of request fulfilment is to:

■ Receive user requests for standard services, and source and deliver required components
■ Provide information about services to users and customers
■ Provide general information and deal with complaints and comments.

The scope of request fulfilment can vary between organizations; some use the service desk to manage service requests alongside incidents, whereas in others there is a separate function.

Whichever approach is used, it must be clear that incidents and service requests are different:

- Incidents occur when something has gone wrong, thus they are unplanned
- Service requests are for additional services, which are planned.

6.2   PROCESS ACTIVITIES, METHODS AND TECHNIQUES (SO 4.3.5)

Request fulfilment is an area in which self-help can improve efficiency. Typical steps for managing a service request include:

- **Menu selection** Users generate service requests via a service management tool with a web interface offering a selection of items from predefined lists. Menus prompt the user for all the required information
- **Financial approval** Standard requests could have pre-agreed fixed prices, otherwise an estimate of cost needs to be submitted for financial approval. Once granted, the request is fulfilled and charges applied (if charging is in place)
- **Other approval** In some cases compliance-related or business approval might also be required
- **Fulfilment** Depending on the request, this is undertaken by the service desk or specialist groups. This could be via a dedicated in-house team or a third party. In all cases the service desk monitors the activity, keeping the user informed of progress
- **Closure** The service request is handed back to the service desk, who confirm that the user is happy with the outcome before the request is closed.

6.3 TRIGGERS, INPUTS, OUTPUTS AND INTERFACES (SO 4.3.6)

The trigger for request fulfilment is the user submitting a service request, either via the service desk or using a self-help facility. This often involves selection from a portfolio of available request types.

The primary interfaces are concerned with requesting services and their subsequent deployment:

- **Service desk/incident management** In the absence of a dedicated function, service requests are received by the service desk and may initially be handled using the incident management process
- **Release and deployment management and SACM** Deployment of many new or changed services will be automated following predefined procedures that include update of the CMS.

6.4 ROLES AND RESPONSIBILITIES (SO 6.6.7)

The roles and responsibilities required are usually undertaken as additional duties for the service desk, change management and service operation functions and/or external suppliers.

These might be assisted by facilities management, procurement and other business areas.

If there are high volumes of service requests, or if they are of critical importance, organizations might have dedicated teams for request fulfilment.

6.5   CHALLENGES, CRITICAL SUCCESS FACTORS AND RISKS (SO 4.3.9)

Challenges for request fulfilment include:

- Clearly defining and documenting the type of request that will be processed through request fulfilment
- Provision of self-help facilities enabling users to interface with the process.

Critical success factors for request fulfilment include:

- Agreement on the services that can be requested, who can request them, and the associated costs involved
- Accessibility of the service, which should be publicized via the service catalogue
- Standard procedures in place for each type of requested service
- Single point of contact for service requests
- Integration of front-end self-help tools with the back-end processes.

Risks for request fulfilment include:

- People unaware of the scope of the request fulfilment process
- Poor user interface
- Back-end process unable to deal with the nature and volume of requests
- Poor metrics due to lack of appropriate monitoring systems.

7   Evaluation

7.1   PURPOSE, GOALS, OBJECTIVES AND SCOPE (ST 4.6.1, 4.6.2)

The purpose of evaluation is to:

■ Provide a consistent way to determine the performance of a service change ('performance' here means all utilities and warranties of the service)

■ Evaluate the actual performance against the expected performance

■ Understand and manage any deviations between expected and actual performance.

The goals of evaluation are to:

■ Evaluate the intended effects of a service change, and as much of the unintended effects as is practical

■ Provide good-quality reports to change management to support effective decisions about whether to approve changes.

The scope of evaluation includes:

■ Evaluation of new or changed services defined by service design, during deployment and before final transition to service operation.

7.2   PROCESS ACTIVITIES, METHODS AND TECHNIQUES (ST 4.6.5)

Key terms used in evaluation are defined in Table 7.1.

Table 7.1 Key terms used in evaluation

Actual performance	The performance achieved following a service change
Capacity	Organization's ability to maintain service capability in defined circumstances
Constraint	Limits on an organization's capacity
Countermeasures	Mitigation that is implemented to reduce risk
Deviations report	A report identifying differences between predicted and actual performance
Evaluation plan	Outcome of the evaluation planning exercise – a plan to perform the evaluation
Evaluation report	A report passed to change management at the end of evaluation. It includes risk profile, deviations report, qualification or validation statements (if applicable) and recommendation
Interim evaluation report	A report passed to change management before the end of evaluation, if there is an unacceptable level of risk
Performance	The utilities and warranties of a service
Performance model	A representation of the performance of a service

Residual risk	The remaining risk after countermeasures have been deployed
Resource	The normal requirements of an organization to maintain service capability
Risk	A function of the likelihood and negative impact of a service not performing as expected
Service capability	Ability of a service to perform as required
Service change	A change to an existing service or the introduction of a new service (a formal definition of service change can be found in section 2.2)
Service design package	Defines the service and provides a plan of service changes over the next period (for example, 12 months). It includes acceptance criteria and predicted performance
Test plan and results	A test plan is a response to an impact assessment. It typically specifies how the change will be tested, what records will be created and where they will be stored etc. It may also include plans for qualification and validation (see section 7.2.3). Test results represent the actual performance following change implementation

Figure 7.1 shows the   aluation process with inputs and outputs.

Figure 7.1 Evaluation process

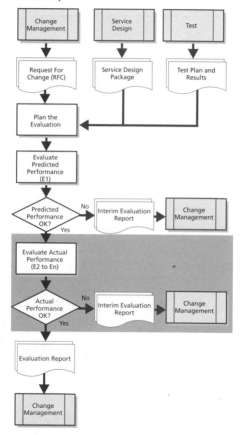

7.2.1   Evaluation plan

Evaluation should be carried out from several different perspectives to help identify unintended as well as intended effects.

7.2.2   Understanding intended and unintended effects of a change

The service design package is analysed to understand the change and the expected benefits. Documentation should make the intended effect clear and include specific measures to determine effectiveness of the change. Intended effects may include some that are detrimental to the service; for example, introducing Sarbanes-Oxley-compliant procedures may add extra steps and costs.

Unintended effects of the change must be identified wherever possible. This may involve discussions with stakeholders and attempts to understand the full impact of the change. Table 7.2 shows factors to be taken into account when considering the predicted effect of a service change.

7.2.3   Evaluation of predicted performance and actual performance

A risk assessment is carried out, based on customer requirements (including acceptance criteria) and predicted performance. If this risk assessment shows unacceptable risks, then an interim evaluation report is created to warn change management, and evaluation activity stops until change management makes a decision.

Table 7.2 Factors for considering the effects of a service change

Factor	Evaluation of service design
S – Service provider capability	Ability of the service provider or service to perform as required
T – Tolerance	Ability or capacity of a service to absorb the change
O – Organizational setting	Ability of the organization to accept the change
R – Resources	Availability of skilled and knowledgeable people, finance, infrastructure, applications and other resources needed to run the service after the change
M – Modelling and measurement	Extent to which predicted performance matches actual behaviour
P – People	The effect of the change on the people
U – Use	Will the service be fit for use? Can warranties be met?
P – Purpose	Will the service be fit for purpose? Can required performance be supported? Will constraints be removed as planned?

After the change has been implemented, a report on actual performance is received from operations staff (or early life support) and another risk assessment is carried out. If this risk assessment shows unacceptable risks, then an interim evaluation report is created to warn change management, and evaluation activity stops until change management makes a decision.

In each case, the risk assessment is based on analysing threats and weaknesses. Risk is calculated as likelihood of event multiplied by impact of event. Risk mitigation may be used to reduce the risk, resulting in a residual risk.

If risks are acceptable, then no interim evaluation report is produced and further analysis is carried out to create an evaluation report. This contains:

- **Deviations report** Comparing actual with predicted performance
- **Risk profile** Showing the residual risk
- **Qualification statement or validation statement (if appropriate)** Formal statement showing compliance with regulations, such as required in defence and pharmaceutical industries. Services and applications may be validated; infrastructure and operating environments may be qualified
- **Recommendation** Advising change management whether to accept or reject the change.

NOTE: An interim evaluation report is produced before the end of evaluation if risks are seen as unacceptable. An evaluation report is only produced at the end of evaluation if risks are acceptable.

7.3 ROLES AND RESPONSIBILITIES (ST 6.3.2.4)

The role of the performance and risk evaluation manager is to:

- Use SDP and release package to develop an evaluation plan to input to service testing
- Establish risks and issues for all aspects of service transition
- Provide evaluation reports (and interim evaluation reports) as input to change management.

7.4 CHALLENGES (ST 4.6.9.1)

Challenges to evaluation include:

- Developing standard performance measures and measurement methods
- Inaccuracy in information supplied by suppliers and projects
- Understanding different stakeholder perspectives
- Managing risk as it affects the overall organization, communicating the approach to risk, and encouraging a risk management culture
- Measuring variation in predictions during and after transition and demonstrating improvement.

8   Knowledge management

8.1   PURPOSE, GOALS, OBJECTIVES AND SCOPE (ST 4.7.1, 4.7.2)

The ability to deliver a quality service or process relies on people understanding the circumstances, options, consequences and benefits of the situation; in other words, their knowledge.

The purpose of knowledge management is to enable organizations to improve the quality of decision making by ensuring that reliable and secure information and data are available.

The objectives of knowledge management include:

■ Enabling the service provider to improve the quality of the service
■ Ensuring staff have a clear and common understanding of the value that services provide to customers
■ Ensuring that, at a given time and location, staff have information on:
  – Who is currently using their services, and the current state of consumption
  – Service delivery constraints and difficulties faced by the customer in fully realizing the benefits expected from the service.

The scope of knowledge management extends to the whole lifecycle and is referenced throughout ITIL:

■ **Inclusions**
  – Oversight of the management of knowledge
  – Information and data from which the knowledge derives

- ■ **Exclusions**
  - – Capture, maintenance and use of service asset and configuration data that remains under the control and management of SACM.

8.2 VALUE TO THE BUSINESS (ST 4.7.3, 4.7.5.4, FIGURE 4.37)

Knowledge management is especially significant within service transition. For example:

- ■ Transitioning knowledge (training) to users, service desk and suppliers
- ■ Awareness of discontinued versions of whatever is to be released
- ■ Establishment of risk and confidence associated with the transition.

Effective knowledge management is a powerful asset for all roles across the service lifecycle.

Implementation of a service knowledge management system (SKMS) helps reduce the cost of maintaining and managing services by increasing the efficiency of operational procedures and reducing risks that arise from the lack of proper mechanisms.

8.3 POLICIES, PRINCIPLES AND BASIC CONCEPTS (ST 4.7.4)

The data-to-information-to-knowledge-to-wisdom structure (DIKW) is shown in Figure 8.1.

Figure 8.1 The flow from data to wisdom

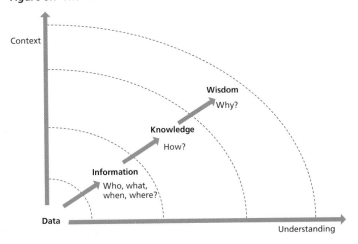

Knowledge management uses the terms data, information, knowledge and wisdom with the following meanings:

- **Data** is facts about events. Most organizations capture massive amounts of data, some of which are stored in structured databases, such as service management and configuration management systems and databases.
- **Information** comes from providing context to data. Information is typically stored in semi-structured formats such as content in documents, spreadsheets and email.

  Knowledge management facilitates capture, query, finding, re-using and learning from information, so that mistakes are not repeated and work is not duplicated.

- **Knowledge** is composed of tacit experiences, ideas and insights, values and judgements of individuals. People gain knowledge both from their own expertise and that of their peers as well as from the analysis of information and data.

  Knowledge is dynamic and context-based. Knowledge transforms information into a format that is 'easy to use'. This is achieved by use of previously collected experiences, awareness and anticipation.

- **Wisdom** uses application and contextual awareness to provide judgement.

8.3.1 The service knowledge management system

Specifically within IT service management, knowledge management will be focused within the SKMS. Underpinning this knowledge will be a considerable quantity of data and information, held in the CMS. Figure 8.2 shows that the SKMS is a broader concept than the CMS, including a much wider base of knowledge, such as:

- The experience of staff
- Records of peripheral matters such as weather reports and organization performance
- Requirements, abilities and expectations of suppliers or users.

8.4   PROCESS ACTIVITIES, METHODS AND TECHNIQUES (ST 4.7.5)

8.4.1 Knowledge management strategy

There should be as wide a span as practicable for knowledge management to incorporate anyone likely to be able to contribute to or benefit from knowledge management.

Figure 8.2 Relationship of the CMDB, CMS and SKMS

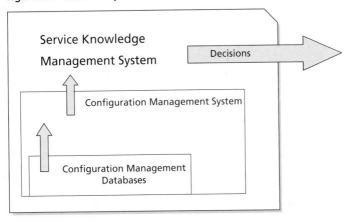

Specifically, knowledge management will identify and plan for the capture of relevant knowledge and the information and data that support it.

8.4.2 Knowledge transfer

During the lifecycle an organization needs to focus on retrieving, sharing and using its knowledge through problem solving, dynamic learning, strategic planning and decision making. Many service management processes and functions will link into this. Links to HR, facilities and other supporting services should also be established, maintained and utilized.

The challenge is getting knowledge transferred between parts of the organization. The knowledge needs to be in a form that is both applicable and easy to use.

If necessary, a gap analysis of knowledge transfer should be undertaken. The output should be a communications improvement plan recognizing that people receive and interpret knowledge in different ways, using different learning styles.

8.4.3 Data and information management

Knowledge rests on the management of the information and data that underpins it. To be efficient, this process needs to have an understanding of some key process inputs such as:

- What data is available
- The cost of capturing and maintaining data
- The value of that data
- How the data and information will be used
- Applicable policies, legislation, standards and other requirements
- Intellectual property and copyright issues.

Often data and information is collected with no clear understanding of how it will be used. Efficiency and effectiveness are delivered by establishing the requirements for information.

In order to make effective use of data in terms of delivering knowledge, a relevant architecture matched to the organization and the knowledge requirements is essential.

Once the requirements have been defined and the architecture set up, data and information management requirements can be established to support knowledge management. For example:

- Information to be collected
- Maintenance of data
- Storage and retrieval
- Backup and recovery
- Publication and usage rights
- Security.

As with all ITIL processes and functions, the capture and use of data and information to support knowledge management needs regular review and attention for continual improvement.

Implementation of an SKMS helps reduce the costs of maintaining and managing services by increasing the efficiency of operational mechanisms whilst reducing the risks that may arise by inaccurate or ineffective mechanisms. Useful materials may include:

- Training materials
- Business process documentation
- Process maps
- Known errors and workarounds
- Business and public calendars.

8.5 TRIGGERS, INPUTS, OUTPUTS AND INTERFACES (ST 4.7.6)

Crucial to the success of knowledge management is the need to ensure that the benefits are understood, supported and embraced by the organization. The success of knowledge management depends on committed support and delivery by everyone involved in service management.

Errors detected during transition will be recorded and analysed. Knowledge of their existence, consequences and workarounds will be made available to service operation staff.

Front-line staff (service desk, second-line support) are the point of capture for service management data. These people must understand that they are also the point of capture for re-usable knowledge. Problem management will typically be users of this collected knowledge and they will usually be responsible for constructing scripts to aid the collection of knowledge within incident management.

Service transition teams will also capture data through all lifecycle phases.

8.6 ROLES AND RESPONSIBILITIES (ST 6.3.2.5)

The knowledge management process owner should be responsible for the following:

- Complying with the organization's policies and processes
- Being the architect of knowledge identification, capture and maintenance
- Ensuring knowledge currency
- Ensuring appropriate accessibility to knowledge
- Monitoring publicity of knowledge, thus supporting the single-repository ethos.

8.7 METRICS AND MEASUREMENT (ST 4.7.7)

Typical metrics for knowledge management are:

- Successful implementation and early-life operation of new or changed services with few knowledge-related errors
- Improved accessibility and management of standards and policies
- Reduced time and effort to support and maintain services
- Reduced time to find diagnostic information for incidents and problems
- Reduced dependency on specific individuals for their personal knowledge
- Number of accesses to the SKMS
- Average time taken to find the knowledge sought

- Errors found in knowledge during audits
- Degree of re-use of materials such as documentation, policies, procedures and service desk scripts
- Trainee satisfaction following training sessions.

Although it is hard to measure the value of knowledge, it is important to determine its value to the organization in order to ensure suitable funding to maintain and improve the knowledge held.

One useful measure of the quality of knowledge transfer is the performance of support groups after a transition. There should be a feedback mechanism to check the understanding and quality of knowledge dissemination.

8.8   RELATIONSHIP WITH CONTINUAL SERVICE IMPROVEMENT (CSI 3.8)

Knowledge management plays a key role in continual service improvement. Each phase of the lifecycle should be capturing data to gain knowledge and understanding, which in turn leads to wisdom. This is frequently referred to as the DIKW model (see Figure 8.1). Organizations often capture data but then fail to format and process this data into information, synthesizing it into knowledge and combining that knowledge with knowledge from others to become wisdom. This applies to services and processes. Therefore knowledge management is pivotal for any improvement.

9 Technology and implementation

9.1 GENERIC REQUIREMENTS FOR ITSM TECHNOLOGY (SO 7.1)

The same technology should be used at all stages of the service lifecycle. Generally this includes:

- **Self-help** With a web front-end offering a menu-driven range of self-help and service requests. Should have a direct interface into the back-end process-handling software
- **Workflow or process engine** To allow definition and control of defined processes such as incident lifecycle, request fulfilment lifecycle and change models. Should allow definition and management of responsibilities, activities, timescales, escalation paths and alerting
- **Integrated CMS** To manage information about all the organization's CIs, together with required attributes and relationships. Should support links to incidents, problems, known errors, change records, release records etc.
- **Discovery/deployment/licensing technology** To populate or verify CMS data and assist in licence management. Can often also be used to deploy software, ideally with an interface to self-help
- **Remote control** To enable support personnel to take control of users' desktops to conduct investigations or correct settings. Must include appropriate security controls
- **Diagnostic utilities** Including scripts and case-based reasoning tools. Ideally should present automated context-sensitive scripts
- **Reporting** Tools should include good reporting capabilities and a means for providing data to industry-standard reporting packages and dashboards

- **Dashboards** To provide 'at a glance' visibility of overall service performance. Displays can also be included in management reports. Dynamic, customized web-based views can be very useful
- **Integration with business service management** To allow combined views of IT service management and business-related IT.

9.2 EVALUATION CRITERIA FOR TECHNOLOGY AND TOOLS (SD 7.2)

The following generic criteria apply to selection of any service management tool:

- Data handling, integration, import, export and conversion
- Data backup, control and security
- Ability to integrate multi-vendor components, existing and future
- Conformity to international open standards
- Usability, scalability and flexibility of implementation and usage
- Support options provided by the vendor, and credibility of the vendor and tool
- Platform the tool will run on and how this fits the IT strategy
- Training and other requirements for customizing, deploying and using the tool
- Initial costs and ongoing costs.

It is generally best to select a fully integrated tool, but this must support the processes used by the organization, and extensive tool customization should be avoided.

Consideration should also be given to the organization's exact requirements. These should be documented in a statement of requirements. Tool requirements should be categorized using MoSCoW analysis:

- **M** – MUST have this
- **S** – SHOULD have this if at all possible
- **C** – COULD have this if it does not affect anything else
- **W** – WON'T have this, but WOULD like in the future.

Each proposed tool can be evaluated against these criteria to ensure the most appropriate tool is selected.

9.3 PRACTICES FOR PROCESS IMPLEMENTATION

Service operation is a stage in the lifecycle and not a separate entity or function. The discussion of processes in this guide has identified typical activities performed on a day-to-day basis by service operation. This section looks at the bigger picture.

9.3.1 Managing change in operations (SO 8.1)

There are many things that could trigger a change in the service operation environment. These include changes to legislation, governance, and business needs, as well as new or upgraded infrastructure and applications.

Service operation staff must be involved in assessment of all changes, not just as members of the CAB but sufficiently early that they can influence design decisions.

The measure of success for any change made to service operation is that customers do not experience any variation or outage. The effects should be invisible, apart from enhanced functionality, quality or financial savings resulting from the change.

9.3.2 Service operation and project management (SO 8.2)

It is important that all projects make use of project management processes. Many organizations treat service operation as 'business as usual' and do not use project management for activities such as major infrastructure upgrades or deployment of new or changed procedures.

Using project management processes can lead to the following advantages:

- Project benefits are agreed and documented
- Increased visibility of what is being done and how it is being managed
- Greater ease of obtaining funding
- Greater consistency and improved quality
- Objectives more likely to be achieved, leading to higher credibility for operational groups.

9.3.3 Assessing and managing risk in service operation (SO 8.3)

Risk assessment and management is required throughout the service lifecycle. There are occasions when assessment of risk to service operation must be carried out and acted on very quickly:

- Assessing the risk of potential changes or known errors
- Failures or potential failures. These may be identified by event management, incident management or problem management, but also by warnings from manufacturers, suppliers or contractors
- Environmental risks. Risks to the physical environment as well as political, commercial or industrial relations risks which could lead to invoking IT service continuity arrangements

- Suppliers, particularly if they control key service components
- Security risks
- Support of new customers or services.

9.3.4 Operational staff in service design and transition (SO 8.4)

Activities during service design and service transition should involve staff from all IT groups to ensure that new components and services are designed, tested and implemented in a way that will provide the service utility and service warranty required.

Service operation staff must be involved during the early stages of design and transition to ensure that new services are fit for purpose from an operational perspective, and supportable in the future. This means:

- Capable of being supported from a technical and operational viewpoint with existing, or agreed additional, resources and skills
- No adverse impact on other practices, processes or schedules
- No unexpected operational costs
- No unexpected contractual or legal complications
- No complex support paths with multiple support departments or third parties.

Planning and implementing changes do not just involve technology. Thought must be given to awareness, cultural change, motivation and many other issues.

9.4 CHALLENGES, CRITICAL SUCCESS FACTORS AND RISKS RELATING TO IMPLEMENTING PRACTICES AND PROCESSES (ST 9.1, 9.2, 9.3)

9.4.1 Challenges

9.4.1.1 Lack of engagement with development and project staff

Many organizations have a separation between operation staff and development staff. This may be deliberate – to avoid collusion leading to security risks – but it may be a source of rivalry.

ITSM is often seen as purely operational, and not needed during development or projects. This can be very damaging as it can lead to a lack of effective planning for how to operate and manage services. The ITIL *Service Design* and *Service Transition* publications describe the steps needed to ensure these issues are considered early enough.

9.4.1.2 Justifying funding

Money spent on service operation is often seen as 'infrastructure costs', with no new business functionality. The ITIL service strategy publication shows how to avoid this perception and ensure an ROI.

Many ITSM investments can save money as well as improving service quality. For example:

- Reduced licence costs due to improved licence management
- Reduced support costs due to fewer incidents and problems, and reduced resolution time
- Reduced headcount due to improved organizational design and better aligned processes reducing duplication of activities
- Less lost business caused by poor IT service quality
- Better utilization of infrastructure leading to deferred purchases.

9.4.1.3 Challenges for service operation managers

Service operation managers have to manage challenges due to the differences between service design and service operation activities. These are typically due to the fact that:

- Service design usually focuses on one service at a time, whereas service operation looks at all services. This operational perspective must be communicated to service design and service transition personnel
- Design is conducted in projects, whereas operation is ongoing. Operation staff may not be available to attend meetings or other activities. This can result in services that are hard to manage and operate. This issue can be overcome by planning for operational staff to be available for project activities
- Service design has metrics that focus on completion to time, to specification and to budget. Ongoing running costs may not be visible until some time after the project completes, at which time service operation personnel are seen as responsible. This should be addressed by active participation of service operation personnel in the service transition, to assess and remedy issues before they affect the operational environment
- Some organizations do not have effective service transition. The role of change management is to schedule deployments, rather than to manage changes. This can only be remedied by implementing robust service transition processes.

9.4.2 Critical success factors

Management support Senior management support is critical for maintaining required funding and resources, as well as visible support when new initiatives are launched.

Middle managers must provide support by following procedures and giving a clear indication that others must do the same, and by hiring required staff.

- **Business support** Business units must understand and support the role they play in adhering to policies, processes and procedures – such as using the service desk to log all requests.

  The business should also agree to costs for implementing service operation and understand the return on investment. This should be done as part of service design, but often is not.

- **Champions** ITSM projects, and the ongoing practices, are often more successful if there are champions who lead others through their enthusiasm and commitment. These champions can be senior managers, but can also succeed if they come from other parts of the organization.

  Champions are often created, or influenced, by formal service management training, particularly at more advanced levels.

  Champions emerge over time; they cannot be created or appointed. Champions must be given time to provide a contribution. Users or customers may be aware of needed improvements from a business perspective, and can be a great help in creating service management processes.

- **Staffing and retention** Projects for new services often underestimate the number of staff required and may not plan for how to retain required skills.

  It is essential to have staff with a good understanding of service management as well as staff with required technical skills. Training staff who then leave for better jobs is not effective, so every service management initiative must include career paths and incentives.

Asking busy staff to take on too many initiatives and new processes can cause service management projects to fail. Use of additional short-term staff can help.

■ **Service management training** In addition to generic service management training, staff should be trained on:
 – The organization's own processes that have been implemented
 – People skills, especially for people in customer-facing positions
 – Understanding the business and the required service culture
 – Service management tools.

Customers and staff also need to be trained on how to work with IT (how to submit access requests, change requests or incidents, how to use self-help etc.).

■ **Suitability of tools** Many processes cannot be performed effectively without suitable tools. Senior management must provide funding for procurement, deployment and ongoing maintenance of these

■ **Validity of testing** Quality of IT services can be enhanced by adequate testing, and provision of good documentation. Sufficient time and effort are needed to plan, design and execute the tests and ideally there should be independent testers

■ **Measurement and reporting** Clear definitions of how things will be measured and reported will provide staff with targets to aim for and allow IT and business managers to review progress and identify opportunities for improvement.

9.4.3 Risks

Many risks are simply the opposite of critical success factors, but the ultimate risk to the business is loss of critical IT services, with subsequent adverse impact on employees, customers and finances.

Risks to operation of services and processes include:

- **Inadequate funding and resources** Funding must be justified, allocated and available
- **Loss of momentum** Service management may be seen as a project. Make clear from the outset that a new way of working is needed
- **Loss of key personnel** Try to cross-train staff and reduce dependencies on individuals
- **Resistance to change** Training, communication and highlighting benefits can help
- **Lack of management support** Middle managers may not gain the hands-on benefits that junior managers do, and may not see the overall vision. Ensure they participate in the overall design, transition and operation.

9.5 PLANNING AND IMPLEMENTING SERVICE MANAGEMENT TECHNOLOGIES (SO 8.5)

There are a number of factors to consider when deploying and implementing ITSM support tools:

- **Licences** The cost of service management tools is usually determined by the type and number of user licences needed. Most tools are modular, so the specific selection of modules also affects the price. Planning the provision of licences is important to avoid unexpected costs. There are a number of different licence types:

- **Dedicated licences** For staff who need frequent and prolonged use of the module (for example, service desk staff)
- **Shared licences** For staff who regularly use the module, with significant times when it is not needed. The ratio of licences to users should be calculated to give sufficient use at acceptable cost
- **Web licences** For staff who need occasional access, or remote access, or only need limited functionality
- **Service on demand** Charge is based on number of hours the service is used. Suitable for smaller organizations or very specialized tools that are not used often. Can also include tools licensed as part of a consulting exercise (for example, for carrying out capacity modelling).

■ **Deployment** Many tools, especially discovery and event monitoring tools, require deployment of clients or agents. This requires careful scheduling, planning and execution and should be subject to formal release and deployment management. Devices may need to be rebooted and this should be planned. Change management should be used and the CMS should be updated.

Particular care should be given to planning deployment to laptops and other portable equipment that may not be connected all the time.

■ **Capacity checks** It may be necessary to check for sufficient system resources (disk space, CPU, memory etc.) when planning a deployment. Allow sufficient lead time for upgrading or replacing equipment. Also check network capacity.

■ **Timing of technology deployment** If tools are deployed too early, they can be seen as 'the solution' and essential process improvements not carried out. If tools are deployed too late, it can be hard to deploy the new process. People need to be trained in use of the tool, as well as the new or updated process, and timing for this must be planned, possibly with additional training after the tools have gone live.

- **Type of introduction** The new tool often replaces an existing tool, and careful planning is needed for the transition. A phased approach is often more appropriate than big bang, but this depends on the exact circumstances. The key factor is planning what data needs to be migrated, and how. If data is being migrated, a data quality audit should be performed. An alternative approach is parallel running, in which case the old tool should run in a 'read only' mode to prevent mistakes.

9.6 TECHNOLOGY FOR IMPLEMENTING COLLABORATION, CONFIGURATION MANAGEMENT AND KNOWLEDGE MANAGEMENT (ST 7.2, 7.3, 7.1)

9.6.1 Collaboration

Collaboration is sharing tacit knowledge and working together to achieve goals. Typical tools to support this include:

- Shared calendars and tasks
- Threaded discussions
- Email and instant messaging
- Whiteboarding, video-conferencing and tele-conferencing.

Communities are a good method for allowing groups spread across countries and time zones to collaborate. The community elects a leader to run the community and subject matter experts to contribute and evaluate knowledge. Tools to support online communities include:

- Community portals
- Email alias management
- Focus groups
- Repository for intellectual property, best practices and work examples
- Online events and net shows.

Recognition for contributions to the community encourages people to share.

Workflow management provides support for managing knowledge through a predefined workflow. This is often used in managing incidents, changes etc. Tools to support this typically provide:

- Workflow design
- Routeing objects and event services
- Gatekeeping at authorization checkpoints and state transition services.

9.6.2 Configuration management

The CMS contains details about the attributes and history of each CI, and details of the important relationships between CIs. Ideally it should be linked to the DML; if this is not possible, then consider automating the comparison of CMS and DML.

The CMS should prevent unauthorized changes to the infrastructure or services. All changes should be recorded, and the status of CIs should be updated automatically if possible. Features that a CMS should provide include:

- Appropriate security controls, only allowing access that is required
- Support for complex CIs with hierarchic and networked relationships and automatic update of version when a component version changes

- Easy addition, modification and deletion of CIs, with automatic validation of input data, automatic detection of relationships where possible, and maintenance of history of all CIs
- Support for model numbers, version numbers and copy numbers
- Support for baselines
- Automatic identification of related CIs when managing incidents, problems and changes
- Good interrogation and reporting, including trend analysis and graphical representation of relationships.

Several tools may need to be integrated to provide a full solution. The CMS may be integrated with the service management system, but integration may be done at the procedural or data level if this is more appropriate. Automated discovery tools can improve efficiency and effectiveness of the CMS.

Ideally, a single tool should manage software assets from the start of systems analysis, but if this is not possible there must be a way to transfer information from development to the live CMS.

9.6.3 Knowledge management

Knowledge management tools support the maintenance of electronic documents and records. A record is evidence of activity, such as minutes of a meeting or details of an incident, problem or change. A document is evidence of intentions, such as policy statements, plans and SLAs.

Knowledge management activities include:

- **Document management** To store, protect, archive, classify and retire documents and information
- **Records management** To store, protect, archive, classify and retire records

- **Content management** To store, maintain and retrieve documents and information on a system or website. Content management makes use of:
    - Web publishing tools, including conferencing, wikis, blogs etc.
    - Word processing, flowcharting and presentation tools
    - Data and financial analysis
    - Publication and distribution
    - Content management systems (codifying, organizing, version control, document architectures).

9.7 THE DEMING CYCLE (CSI 3.6, 3.7, 5.5)

Planning and implementing service management technologies is not a project that ends; it is part of the process for supporting and improving the overall service management system.

The Deming Cycle, shown in Figure 9.1, is a four-stage cycle for quality improvement. The cycle is based on a process-led approach to management, with defined processes, measurement of activities and audited outputs.

The four stages of the Deming Cycle are:

- **Plan** Document scope, goals and objectives; identify processes, tools or whatever else is to be developed and deployed; define measurement systems; establish timelines and resources
- **Do** Obtain the funding; carry out detailed design work; document the processes, roles and responsibilities; carry out training and communication; deploy the new process or tool. The Do stage also includes ongoing running of the new process or tool

Figure 9.1 The Deming Cycle

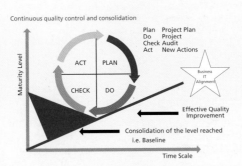

- **Check** Monitor, measure and review, to ensure that the goals and objectives are being met. This includes reporting against plans, and conducting process assessments and audits. The key output of this stage should be identification of opportunities for improvement
- **Act** This stage is where improvements are actually implemented. This could include updating policies, processes, procedures, roles and responsibilities, tools, documents etc.

10   Qualifications

10.1   OVERVIEW

The ITIL V3 Qualification Scheme has four levels:

- Foundation level
- Intermediate level (Lifecycle and Capability streams)
- ITIL Expert
- ITIL Master.

Candidates gain credits for each examination taken, leading to an ITIL Expert certificate (22 credits). The ITIL Master certificate is in development.

10.2   FOUNDATION

The foundation level ensures candidates gain knowledge of the ITIL terminology, structure and basic concepts, and comprehend the core principles of ITIL practices for service management. Foundation represents two credits towards the ITIL Expert.

Figure 10.1 The ITIL V3 Qualification Scheme

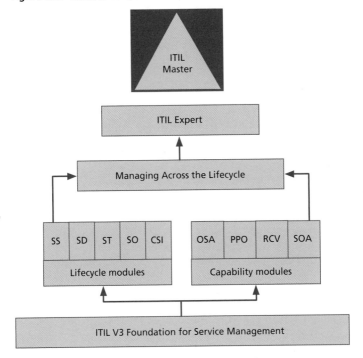

10.3   INTERMEDIATE LEVEL

There are two streams in the intermediate level, assessing an individual's ability to analyse and apply concepts of ITIL:

- **Lifecycle stream** Built around the five core publications, for candidates wanting to gain knowledge within the service lifecycle context. Each module achieves three credits
- **Capability stream** Built around the four practitioner-based clusters, for candidates wanting to gain knowledge of specific processes and roles. Each module achieves four credits:
  - **Operational support and analysis** Including event, incident, problem and access management, and request fulfilment processes; service desk, technical, IT operations and application management functions.
  - **Planning, protection and optimization** Including capacity, availability, service continuity, information security and demand management processes
  - **Service offerings and agreement** Including service portfolio, service level, service catalogue, demand, supplier and financial management
  - **Release, control and validation** Including change, release and deployment, service asset and configuration, and knowledge management, request fulfilment, service validation and testing, and evaluation processes

Candidates may take units from either of the streams to accumulate credits.

To complete the intermediate level, the Managing Across the Lifecycle course (five credits) is required to bring together the full essence of a lifecycle approach to service management, consolidating knowledge gained across the qualification scheme.

10.4   ITIL EXPERT

Candidates automatically qualify for an ITIL Expert certificate once they have achieved the pre-requisite 22 credits from foundation (mandatory initial unit) and intermediate units (including Managing Across the Lifecycle, mandatory final unit). No further examinations or courses are required.

10.5   ITIL MASTER

Although not yet finalized, this qualification is intended to assess an individual's ability to apply and analyse the ITIL V3 concepts in new areas.

10.6   EXISTING ITIL V1 AND V2 QUALIFICATIONS

The ITIL V3 Qualification Scheme has bridging courses for those candidates with existing ITIL (V1 and V2) qualifications. An existing ITIL V1 or V2 Foundation qualification equates to 1.5 credits, and successfully passing a V3 Foundation Bridge course provides the further 0.5 credits required to progress to the intermediate level.

A V1 or V2 Manager qualification equates to 17 credits, and successfully passing a V3 Manager Bridge course provides the further five credits required to achieve the ITIL Expert certificate.

There are also credits for the V2 practitioners, either 2 credits for single processes or 3.5 for clustered processes. A candidate with more than 12 credits from foundation and V2 practitioner courses may take the V3 Manager Bridge and the Managing Across the Lifecycle exams to qualify as an ITIL Expert. Candidates with fewer practitioner credits may combine these with ITIL V3 Lifecycle and Capability exams, and Managing Across the Lifecycle, to achieve ITIL Expert.

Figure 10.2 The ITIL V3 Bridging Qualification Scheme

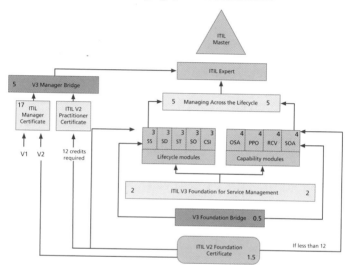

There are also complementary qualifications that are awarded credits under this scheme. The number of credits for each qualification can be found in the credit profiler at:

www.itil-officialsite.com/itilservices/V1/map.asp

Further information

RELATED STANDARDS AND OTHER SOURCES

ITIL provides advice and guidance on best practice relating to the provision of IT services. The following public frameworks and standards are relevant:

- ISO/IEC 20000: IT Service Management
- ISO/IEC 27001: Information Security Management (ISO/IEC 17799 is the corresponding code of practice)
- ISO/IEC 14001: Environmental Management
- ISO/IEC 15504: Software Process Improvement and Capability Determination (SPICE)
- ISO/IEC 19770 (software asset management)
- ISO/IEC 38500 (governance)
- Capability Maturity Model Integration (CMMI®)
- Control Objectives for Information and related Technology (COBIT®)
- Projects in Controlled Environments (PRINCE2™)
- Project Management Body of Knowledge (PMBOK®)
- Management of Risk (M_o_R®)
- eSourcing Capability Model for Service Providers (eSCM-SP™)
- Telecom Operations Map (eTOM®)
- Six Sigma™.

Organizations need to integrate guidance from multiple frameworks and standards.

The primary standard for IT service management is ISO/IEC 20000. The standard and ITIL are aligned and continue to be aligned, although the standard is soon to be extended with the development of parts 3 and 4:

- ISO/IEC 20000-1:2005 Part 1: Specification (defines the requirements for service management)
- ISO/IEC 20000-2:2005 Part 2: Code of Practice (provides guidance and recommendations on how to meet the requirements in part 1)
- ISO/IEC 20000-3 Part 3: Scoping and Applicability (not available yet)
- ISO/IEC 20000-4 Part 4: Service Management Process Reference Model (not available yet)
- BIP 0005: A Manager's Guide to Service Management
- BIP 0015: IT Service Management: Self-assessment Workbook (currently assesses against ITIL V2, to be revised via ITIL V3 complementary publications).

These documents provide a standard against which organizations can be assessed and certified with regard to the quality of their IT service management processes.

An ISO/IEC 20000 certification scheme was introduced in December 2005. The scheme was designed by the itSMF UK and is operated under its control. A number of auditing organizations are accredited within the scheme to assess and certify organizations as compliant with the ISO/IEC 20000 standard and its content.

FURTHER GUIDANCE AND CONTACT POINTS

TSO

PO Box 29
Norwich NR3 1GN
United Kingdom
Tel: +44(0) 870 600 5522
Fax: +44(0) 870 600 5533
Email: customer.services@tso.co.uk
www.tso.co.uk

OGC

Rosebery Court
St Andrews Business Park
Norwich NR7 0HS
United Kingdom
Tel: +44(0) 845 000 4999
Email: ServiceDesk@ogc.gsi.gov.uk
www.itil.co.uk

itSMF Ltd

150 Wharfedale Road
Winnersh Triangle
Wokingham
Berkshire RG41 5RB
United Kingdom
Tel: +44(0) 118 918 6500
Fax: +44(0) 118 969 9749
Email: service@itsmf.co.uk
www.itsmf.co.uk

APM Group Limited

Sword House
Totteridge Road
High Wycombe
Buckinghamshire HP13 6DG
United Kingdom
Tel: +44(0) 1494 452 450
Fax: +44(0) 1494 459 559
Email: servicedesk@apmgroupltd.com
www.apmgroupltd.com

Best practice with ITIL

The ITIL V3 publication portfolio consists of a unique library of titles that offer guidance on quality IT services and best practices. These titles include:

- The ITIL lifecycle suite (core publications) which comprise:
    - Service Strategy
    - Service Design
    - Service Transition
    - Service Operation
    - Continual Service Improvement
    - The Official Introduction to the ITIL Service Lifecycle
- Key element guides (pocket-sized reference books based on the core publications)
- Passing your ITIL Foundation Exam
- Passing your ITIL Intermediate Stream Exam
- An Introductory Overview of ITIL V3
- ITIL V3 Foundation Handbook
- Operational Support and Analysis ITIL V3 Intermediate Capability Handbook
- Release, Control and Validation ITIL V3 Intermediate Capability Handbook

About itSMF

The itSMF is the only truly independent and internationally recognized forum for IT service management professionals worldwide. This not-for-profit organization is a prominent player in the ongoing development and promotion of IT service management best practice, standards and qualifications, and has been since 1991.

Globally, the itSMF now boasts more than 6,000 member companies, blue-chip and public-sector alike, covering in excess of 70,000 individuals spread over 50+ international chapters.

Each chapter is a separate legal entity and is largely autonomous. itSMF International provides an overall steering and support function to existing and emerging chapters. It has its own website at www.itsmfi.org

The UK chapter has in excess of 16,000 members: it offers a flourishing annual conference, online bookstore, regular regional meetings, special-interest groups and numerous other benefits for members. Its website is at www.itsmf.co.uk.

About Best Management Practice

UK government and best practice

The Office of Government Commerce (OGC), as an office of HM Treasury, plays a vital role in developing methodologies, processes and frameworks and establishing these as best practice.

The huge growth in the market for OGC's best-practice guidance is evidence of how highly it is valued – proving that it offers not just theory but workable business solutions. ITIL is now the most widely accepted approach to service management in the world, while PRINCE2 has established itself as a global leader in project management.

OGC, on behalf of the UK government, remains committed to maintaining and developing the guidance. Through an innovative and successful partnering arrangement, OGC is able to ensure that users are supported by high-quality publications, training, qualification schemes and consultancy services.

OGC and its official partners

In 2006, OGC completed an open competitive procurement and appointed The Stationery Office (TSO) as official publisher and the APM Group Ltd (APMG) as official accreditor. Together they have created Best Management Practice as the official home of OGC's best-practice guidance. The partners are committed to delivering, supporting and endorsing the very best products and services in the marketplace.

The Stationery Office (TSO)

TSO draws upon more than 200 years of print and publishing services experience, and is the only official publisher for OGC's best-practice guidance.

TSO also manages the various refresh projects on OGC's behalf and ensures that the quality of the guidance is maintained at the highest possible level. A dedicated team serves the Best Management Practice community, providing newsletters, updates and latest information on the products and current projects.

APM Group (APMG)

APMG is a global business providing accreditation and certification services. It is one of the first medium-sized companies to establish an independent Ethics and Standards Board to monitor its business practice and to help ensure it supports the industries it serves in a transparent and responsible way.

APMG has been instrumental in helping to establish PRINCE2 as an international standard and now provides global accreditation schemes in ITIL, PRINCE2, MSP™ (Managing Successful Programmes) and M_o_R (Management of Risk).

Keep up to date with Best Management Practice

The Best Management Practice Knowledge Centre brings together the official partners and recognized user groups to create a comprehensive source of information. Here you can find articles, White Papers, book reviews and events, as well as links to the individual product sites.

Visit www.best-management-practice.com